# WATERMELON WINE

## *The Spirit of Country Music*

# FRYE GAILLARD

# WATERMELON WINE

## The Spirit of Country Music

St. Martin's Press    New York

**Library of Congress Cataloging in Publication Data**

Gaillard, Frye.
  Watermelon wine.

  1.  Country-music—United States—History and criticism.  I.  Title.
ML3561.C69G34      784      76-62766
ISBN 0-312-85697-0

*To Rosemary, Rachel, Tracy, Bonnie and Alexander*

# Acknowledgments

Though I didn't know it at the time, this book began in March of 1974 when I was assigned by *Southern Voices* magazine to do an article on the Grand Ole Opry and the future of country music. I had never written about country music before, and had only a layman's familiarity with what it's all about. In the course of doing the article, however, I was fortunate to talk at length with singing star Waylon Jennings, songwriter Vince Matthews, and a remarkable Nashville minister named Will D. Campbell. Borrowing heavily from their ideas, I wrote an article that attracted a good deal of attention and prompted several people—including my writer friends John Egerton, Lawrence Wright, Steve Nickeson and Alex Bontemps—to urge me to expand it into a book.

Once the idea had taken hold of me, I received invaluable advice and assistance from many different quarters. Country musicians like George Hamilton IV, Clay and Arthur Smith, Mickey Newbury, Michael Murphey, Mike Kosser, Dick Feller, Bobby Braddock, and Guy and Susanna Clark went out of their way to be helpful. So did Loyal Jones, an Appalachian folklorist who is brimming with insight and information about the early years of hillbilly music; and Mike Tolleson of the Armadillo World Headquarters, who was a valuable contact in researching the chapter on Austin, Texas.

I also profited from other people's writings: Bill C. Malone's *Country Music USA*, Johnny Cash's *Man in Black*, and Roger M. Williams's thorough biography of Hank Williams, *Sing a Sad Song*. In addition, I was able to tap into the knowledge of magazine writers such as Pete Axthelm of *Newsweek*, Chet Flippo of *Rolling Stone*, and Michael Bane and Patrick Carr of *Country Music*.

The biggest debts of all, however, are owed to my friends. Polly Paddock, a talented writer and valued soul sister from *The Charlotte Observer*, read and criticized every chapter as it came off the typewriter. Chapter Ten was an outgrowth of a newspaper article that Michael Bane and I wrote together. And several other writers—Lew Powell, Frank Barrows and John Egerton—read major segments and offered advice and reassurance.

There were some nonwriters too. Doug Marlette and Florence Tuggle were my number-one cheerleading team throughout, and Carol Lynn McCarty and Jack and Pam Swinney offered encouragement at critical junctures.

The editors of *The Charlotte Observer* were extremely generous in affording me time to work on the book, and in publishing several chapters of it. Other segments were published at *Country Music, Southern Exposure* and the *Louisville Courier-Journal Sunday Magazine,* and I profited from the editing suggestions I received along the way.

In addition, I'm deeply grateful to my editor, Julie Garriott, and her colleagues at St. Martin's Press for their sensitive handling of the book once it was completed.

But most important of all, of course, was my wife and best friend, Rosemary. Since she alone saw the product in its prepolished state, it was her unpleasant duty to tell me when it wasn't any good. She did, and eventually, I hope, it got a little better.

F.G.

# CONTENTS

# INTRODUCTION

The song is true. It tells of a shadowy, melancholy night in a near-empty lounge. There were only three people in the place—a sleepy-eyed bartender glancing at a television that sputtered nearby; an old black man pushing a broom around the clusters of nearby chairs; and a stocky, round-faced songwriter pouring down impressive quantities of top-grade whiskey.

There is usually a folksy formality about such situations—an unwritten code that nobody speaks to anybody else except in the tones of casual, unprobing anonymity. The soft-spoken songwriter fit in well. His name was Tom T. Hall, a young man from Olive Hill, Kentucky, who had composed a million-selling hit for Jeannie C. Riley, an off-beat ballad called "Harper Valley PTA." Hall is a quiet, contemplative sort of fellow, but on this particular evening his contemplations were to be interrupted.

The old black janitor ambled in his direction and struck up a conversation that broke all the rules. It proved to be highly personal, for one thing, and also unsolicited, the old man rambling on in cheerful, twinkly-eyed indifference to Hall's apparent preference for solitude. But there is something to be said for sharing wisdom with a stranger. The old man knew it, and deep down so did Hall. In the end, the barriers crumbled, and the old man's insights became fodder for a song.

This is the heart of Hall's recollections:

**There wasn't anyone around, 'cept this old man and me**
**The guy who ran the bar was watching "Ironsides" on TV**
**Uninvited, he sat down and opened up his mind**
**On old dogs and children and watermelon wine.**

**Ever had a drink of watermelon wine? he asked**
**He told me all about it, though I didn't answer back**
**Ain't but three things in this world that's worth a solitary dime**
**But old dogs and children and watermelon wine.**

**Old dogs care about you even when you make mistakes**
**And God bless little children while they're still too young to hate.**
**When he moved away I found my pen and copied down that line**
**'Bout old dogs and children and watermelon wine... ©**

Because of lyrics like that, Tom T. Hall has emerged as one of the best country composers of the 1970s. He has a remarkable ability to ferret out the feelings of average people in everyday situations—which is, more than anything else, the quality that defines good country songs.

The people who have mastered that quality vary widely in the backgrounds they bring to the task. Kris Kristofferson was a Rhodes Scholar. Alex Harvey, who wrote the Tanya Tucker hit "Delta Dawn," has his master's degree in music. But far more common are the self-taught veterans of a different kind of life—people like Doug and Rusty Kershaw, a couple of dirt-poor Cajun boys from southern Louisiana.

The Kershaws were still children when they began their career as professional musicians. Their early start was assured one day when little Rusty, who wasn't even ten, ducked into the houseboat where the family lived and was greeted by a horrifying sight—his father lying bloody on the floor, his arm draped limply and accidentally across the stock of a shotgun.

The suicide of Papa Kershaw was a devastating event for a no-luck Cajun family in the waning days of the Depression. But there was nothing to do but carry on, and Mama Rita Kershaw, on her own now with young sons to raise, pulled out the old accordion she had used to while away the time in the afternoons, her kids chasing fireflies in the summer dusk; and she went to work in the speak-easies and honky-tonks that abound in the swamplands west of New Orleans.

It was a hard life, but not a lonely one, for Mrs. Kershaw soon brought her sons into the act. For the boys, and especially for Rusty, it was the beginning of a see-saw musical career that has sent them spinning from the bottom to the top and back again on more than one occasion. As teenagers they made it big on "Louisiana Hayride," a Saturday-night radio show produced out of Shreveport on station KWKH. They were in good company there. It was the place where Hank Williams got his start, where he was performing when he died, and where his son, Hank, Jr., made his professional debut.

But the Kershaw boys were nothing if not ambitious, and they eventually left to become regulars on the Grand Ole Opry, producing the kind of hard-driving, foot-stomping bayou music they had learned as children in the Louisiana low country.

In the early Sixties, however, the act began to have its problems. Rusty, the crazier of the two in those days (which is quite a distinction in the relative scheme of things), began dipping heavily into alcohol and drugs, consuming several fifths of gin and whiskey each day and managing to avoid passing out by swallowing a steady diet of amphetamines. Periodically they would ship him off to the alcoholics hospital in Madison, Tennessee, where he would dry out, receive his discharge, and begin to repeat the process.

It was on one of those trips to Madison that Rusty got the idea for a song that, in its simplicity, cut right through to the central reality of his own life and, no doubt, the lives of thousands of country music fans. The song, entitled "That Don't Leave Much Time to Fool Around," is a kind of plaintive warning about the inexorability of time, and the innumerable possibilities for wasting it. This is partly how it goes:

**First you start with walking, then you gotta think about talking**
**Slowly you form a meaning of what is said.**
**Along with the pain of growing, learning things about knowing,**
**That don't leave much time to fool around...**

**Love has a way of growing, there's a baby on the way**
**Soon you'll be a father, she's in the family way.**
**Don't blink an eye while your child's growing**
**Cause you're not here to stay**
**And that don't leave much time to fool around.** ©

It's doubtful that Kershaw set out to strike any cosmic chords. Like most country composers, he simply writes what he feels. But he's good at it, and so are dozens of others.

You have to drop your guard a little if you're not really used to it . . . let your emotions run a bit more free. But when Hank Williams tells what it's like to be lonesome, or Barbara Fairchild laments the inevitable estrangement between a mother and a teenage daughter, or Bill Anderson compares the squalor of big city neon to the natural beauty of the stars, there is a potency about country music that more and more people are coming to appreciate.

The worst of it is positively awful; simplicity can sometimes be a curse. But at its best, it tells us a lot about ourselves (sometimes more than we want to know), and *Watermelon Wine* looks at how it does that.

The music has changed enormously in the last several decades. It had to. Its fans have lived through wars, depressions, recessions, civil rights upheavals, polarization, scandals and changing sexual and religious values; and all those things have affected the music. It was inevitable that they would, for the country sound has always served a function larger than simple entertainment. Whether it's the honky-tonking laments of Lefty Frizzell (or more recently, Moe Bandy or Gary Stewart), or whether it's Guy Clark writing about a dying wino and a Dallas whore, there is an urgency of feeling about country music—a relentlessly accurate reflection of whatever emotion is being portrayed.

No longer, however, do the feelings trace directly and simply to predictable origins. A new generation of country performers has wandered into Nashville, young men and women who draw their inspiration from a bewildering array of influences.

Dick Feller is a typical example. He's a thirtyish, baby-faced songwriter from Bronough, Missouri, whose biggest hit was a novelty number called "The Credit Card Song." More than many of his contemporaries, Feller is articulate and philosophical when he talks about the people who have shaped his craft. He points first to the obvious influences—Johnny Cash, Merle Travis, Chet Atkins, Jimmy Rodgers. But there were also, he says, the jazzmen—Miles Davis, Gerry Mulligan—and the people who sang the blues—Jimmy Reed, Bobby Bland and John Lee Hooker.

In addition, Feller cites about half a dozen poets, from W. H. Auden to Gwendolyn Brooks; and it is no accident, he argues, that John Steinbeck once wrote a foreword for a Woody Guthrie song-book.

But if the Nashville picker-poets no longer come from pockets of utter isolation—if Doc Watson's son, Merle, is strongly influenced by Eric Clapton and other sure-fingered rock guitarists—it is also true that the power of tradition was never more alive than it is in today's country music. One of Waylon Jennings's biggest hits was an ode to Hank Williams, and one of the most popular nightspots in Nashville is a downtown hole-in-the-wall called the Old Time Pickin' Parlor. There, on a given Saturday night, you can find young Appalachian musicians like Norman Blake pouring out crystal-pure hillbilly music that's so old-fashioned it calls up visions of a European reel.

The tension between tradition and change has become a creative, dominating force in country music, just as it has shaped the lives of the people who listen. But there is another dialectic that's also at work, and the effects of this one are far less hopeful. Because of the growing mass demand for country music, a high-pressure industry has grown up to produce it, and it finds itself caught up in the modern, all-American rush toward faddism and mass production.

The tug-of-war between commercialism and creativity is a crucial struggle throughout the music world, and nowhere has it been more bitterly fought than within Nashville's most venerated institution, the Grand Ole Opry. That's where this book begins.

# WATERMELON WINE

## The Spirit of Country Music

# 1

# COMMERCIALIZING THE HERITAGE:
## The Grand Ole Opry

**Walk out of this bar**
**Turn the radio on in my car**
**And listen to that Grand Ole Opry show©**

*—Hoyt Axton*

People disagree about Jimmy Snow. Some say he's a holy man, and some say he's just another of those dime-a-dozen radio God-salesmen who have made a pretty fair living off the souls of Southern white people for almost as long as men have known about the airwaves. But whatever he is, it didn't much matter on the night of March 15, 1974, for the spirit was moving inside Jimmy Snow, and there was a fire in his belly and a quiver in his voice. He knew it was his kind of crowd, and knew too that there might never be another one quite like it. He was ready.

Jimmy Snow had heard the call of the Lord, he explained, one cold winter night a dozen years before, when he had found himself in his front yard, alone and on his knees, no shirt on his back, listening to voices from above. Because of that night, and because his daddy happens to be Hank Snow, a pillar of the Grand Ole Opry for decades, it fell to Reverend Jimmy to preach maybe the last sermon that would ever be heard in Nashville's ramshackled old Ryman Auditorium. The Ryman is a creaky, magnificent monument to a lot of things—to the conscience of Tom Ryman for one; for it was Ryman, a hard-living, liquor-dispensing riverboat operator, who had had his own encounter with the Divinity a little less than a century ago and decided to build a downtown tabernacle to honor the event.

In the years that followed, Ryman's brick and stained-glass edifice shook with the thunder of many an evangelist, and the crowds would swarm in on muggy summer evenings to listen to Billy Sunday and the rest of them, shouting their amens and standing up for Jesus. But gradually economics got mixed into the picture, and the Ryman Auditorium evolved into an entertainment center—a metamorphosis culminating in 1943 in the Grand Ole Opry's choice of the Ryman for its permanent quarters.

There was logic in the choice, of course. For the same people who had come to hear Billy Sunday were just as likely to come hear Hank Snow and Roy Acuff and Sam McGee. They felt comfortable there, and for upwards of thirty years they arrived in droves.

But March 15, 1974, marked the end of that era. It was the Opry's last performance in its old home, and when it moved on the following evening, the President of the United States came down to celebrate, and the crowd that was there to celebrate with him consisted not of the poor whites whose music was being performed onstage, but of the Nashville business people, who appreciated the economic possibilities if not the twanging guitars.

The night before, however, had belonged to Jimmy Snow and the country people. And in place of the President, there was Johnny Cash in his ruffled white shirt and long-tailed coat—looking like a Civil War-vintage U.S. senator, but singing like what he is: a man who has seen both the bottom and the top, and who was probably right at home in both places.

Cash was the closing act for Jimmy Snow's "Grand Ole Gospel Time,"

Tootsie Bess, the feisty, beloved proprietor of Tootsie's Orchid Lounge, has gained as much fame in recent years as the musicians whose photos line her walls. (Photo by Bruce Cooter, courtesy *The Nashville Tennessean*.)

Jimmy Snow exhorts the late night faithful at the Ryman Auditorium's final show, urging them to stand up for Jesus and America. (Photo by George L. Walker III.)

Instamatic cameras have become a way of life at The Grand Ole Opry, and at country music performances all over America. (Photo by Bruce Cooter, courtesy *The Nashville Tennessean*.)

Moonlight washes over the Ryman Auditorium as the fans make their way to the door. (Photo by Jim McGuire.)

A broad grin settles on the face of veteran guitar picker Sam McGee, as he heads toward the stage of The Grand Ole Opry. (Photo by George L. Walker III.)

a popular Friday-night feature of the Opry, and that night's show was one of the best. It featured the traditional gospel renditions of the LeFevres, the more upbeat compositions of a young Johnny Cash protege named Larry Gatlin, a rollicking, foot-stomping performance by country-rock singer Dobie Gray (who is one of the few blacks ever to appear at the Opry), and then the whole Cash clan.

By the time Dobie Gray was through it was late at night, and though it was cold and rainy outside, it was stuffy and humid within. The air was musty with mingled sweat fumes, and the people were tired. But they came abruptly to life and the flashbulbs popped like a psychedelic light show when Cash appeared on stage. And when he and his venerated mother-in-law, Mama Maybelle Carter, led the entire cast through the country-folk classic "Will the Circle Be Unbroken?" even the hard-bitten newspaper reporters in the crowd had to admit they were probably seeing something special. At least a few eyes were not entirely dry.

Then Cash left the stage and Jimmy Snow, as is his custom late in the show, launched into his Friday-night fire-and-brimstone message— mingling his exhortations for Jesus and America and the good ole days, and forgetting, it seemed, that immortal sermons don't have to be eternal.

Meanwhile, a very different scene was taking place across the alley from the Opry's backstage door—in the beer-sloshing pandemonium of Tootsie's Orchid Lounge.

Tootsie's is a typical-looking downtown dive with a garish purple front, presumably approximating the color of an orchid. In the front window are two neon Stroh's Beer signs, one of which works. Neighboring establishments include a pawnshop, a skin-flick theater, and the Magic Touch Massage Parlor, which generally finds itself locked in a chronic life-and-death struggle with the local D.A. The inside walls of Tootsie's are papered with thousands of photographs and autographs of musicians, ranging in stature from Elvis Presley and Faron Young to such lesser lights as Billy Troy and Ken Allen.

As its inner decor suggests, the thing that sets Tootsie's apart is its clientele. Over the years, country musicians have made it a part of their ritual to duck out the back door of the Opry House and grab a quick beer with Tootsie—rubbing shoulders in the process with the truck drivers, downtown drunks, Opry fans, and other everyday beerdrinkers who are, in fact, the blood and guts of country music.

The first time I was a part of that scene was around 1971, when I was with a group of half a dozen tourists that happened to include several high-powered newspaper editors from my home state of Alabama. Our table was being attended by an enormously obese waitress, who reminded me somehow of the Wife of Bath and regaled us with a wide assortment of mildly off-color jokes. As she served the second round of beers, she placed one of them too close to the edge of the table. It teetered precariously for a moment, then toppled neatly into one of the editorial laps. "Oops," she said matter-of-factly in her flattest cracker twang, "did I get it on your dick?"

The editor stared helplessly from his lap to the waitress and back to his lap, trying to decide what response was appropriate under the circumstances. And then with his pretensions pretty well devastated, he collapsed in helpless laughter. It was typical of the sort of ribald egalitarianism that prevails at Tootsie's, presided over by Tootsie herself—Tootsie Bess, a worldly-wise little lady who is known around Nashville for her acts of maternal kindness toward anyone down on his luck.

Tootsie's is one of those collateral country music institutions that have nurtured the Grand Ole Opry for years. And though such things are difficult to measure, the Opry is somehow a little bit different now that it has moved from its old building and severed its back-alley affiliation with the orchid-colored lounge.

The lounge itself, to the surprise of a few people around Nashville, has developed enough institutional momentum over the years to survive very nicely. The crowds, though smaller than they used to be, are still respectable, and the only difference is that Tootsie's one-of-a-kind jukebox—which she still crams full of songs from the lesser-knowns as well as the stars—now competes with live, hard-country bands on Saturday evenings.

But if a sizeable handful of Opry fans have refused to abandon Tootsie's or their other traditional stomping grounds like Ernest Tubbs's Record Shop across the street, it is also true that the biggest crowds have shifted their allegiance to the Opry's new home. By any objective standards of comparison, the new place is a great deal nicer than the Ryman. It is bigger, it has more comfortable seats, its acoustics are more scientifically coordinated; and it's in what would be an idyllic pastoral setting on the winding banks of the Cumberland River. The only problem is that the Opry people also plopped a large amusement park down on the same spot, and it doesn't quite fit. It's a nice amusement park, with a hell of a roller coaster and a lot of animals and things for the kids to look at; but its connotations are overwhelmingly 1970s-American and partake little of the beer-guzzling, God-fearing milieu of white-man's soul that used to surround the Ryman.

The Opry folks, however, seem to like it. The press kit handed out to reporters on hand for the grand opening was jammed full of quotes from various stars on the virtues of Opryland, as the new place is called: "I am very much impressed with the structure of the new Opry House," said Roy Acuff. "I think it is the greatest thing that has happened since the Grand Ole Opry was born," added Roy Drusky. "The move will be a great thing for country music," offered Hank Snow. And so on.

No doubt the quotes were for real, but whether they were or not, nobody could deny that the Opry got off to a spectacular start the first night in its new home. On hand among others for the dedication performance were one President, two senators, at least three governors, and a basketful of congressmen. The President, who clearly enjoyed his temporary retreat from the pressures of Watergate, played "God Bless America" on the piano. Roy Acuff tried unsuccessfully to teach him how to yo-yo. And the specially invited crowd, which was a Nixon crowd—not country, but spiffy, big-business, fund-raising Republican—loved every minute of it.

The Opry performers themselves were in pretty glittery form. Comedian Jerry Clower told some of his funniest down-home Mississippi stories. Porter Waggoner was dressed in one of his gaudiest sequined suits. And blond-haired Jeannie Sealy offered a knock-out version of "Don't Touch Me If You Don't Love Me, Sweetheart," dressed at the time in a svelte, tight-fitting pants suit, with a bare midriff and the kind of plunging neckline that would have knocked many a country matron dead in her tracks from shock.

Backstage the reporters were swarming around, snatching interviews where they could, and during the course of it all, a Voice of America man cornered Minnie Pearl just outside her dressing room. "Would you tell us, please," he said, "if you think perhaps that the Grand Ole Opry has lost its innocence?"

Minnie Pearl paused thoughtfully before answering, for contrary to her "Howdeee" public image, she is an enormously intelligent woman. "Well," she said quietly, "there are a lot of people who would argue that the Opry lost its innocence some time ago back when the music started to change."

"Lordy, I reckon it has changed," echoed Sam McGee, and he had ample reason to know. McGee, then 79 years old and the oldest performer on the show, joined the Opry on its third or fourth radio broadcast back in 1925, when it was still called "The WSM Barn Dance" and performed in a small hotel room. Those were the days when country music was in its commercial infancy. Record producers and radio broadcasters were just beginning to grapple with the notion that an art form as crude and backwoodsy as hillbilly music could have any sort of commercial possibilities. A few of the producers, in moments of studied open-mindedness, could appreciate the fiddlers and the glib-fingered guitar and banjo pickers, but the singers—with their sentimental lyrics and piercing harmonies—simply could not be taken seriously.

But at one radio station, WSB in Atlanta, that point of view crumbled quite rapidly in the late spring of 1922. Soon after the station went on the air in mid-March, it began to feature country performances by such artists as the Reverend Andrew Jenkins, a blind gospel singer, and Fiddling John Carson, a high-pitched vocalist who later become one of the first country musicians to record commercially.

The audience response to these programs was heartening, to say the least, and the same was true the following year, some fifteen hundred miles to the west in Fort Worth, Texas. On January 4, 1923, station WBAP featured an hour and a half's worth of square-dance music by a spirited fiddler and Confederate veteran named M. J. Bonner. WBAP had not been on the air very long, but never in its brief history had it received so many ecstatic phone calls from listeners demanding more of the same. As a result, the station soon began a regular program—reportedly heard as far away as New York and Hawaii—called "The WBAP Barn Dance."

At about this time, record companies began getting into the act—but almost by accident. Seeking an antidote for plunging sales, recording director Ralph Peer of Okeh records in New York began putting on tape a number of urban blues musicians who, along with scores of other blacks, had migrated north in the years following World War I. The experiment met with immediate success, and Peer ventured south in the hope of recording still more blues musicians in the quainter confines of their native habitat. His travels took him to places like Atlanta and station WSB, and there he discovered and decided to record the other side of the Southern folk scene—country-singing white artists like Fiddling John Carson.

Other record companies soon followed suit, and in the late twenties and early thirties the number of country records on the market began to proliferate rapidly. A few ministars emerged—people like Pop Stoneman and Charlie Poole—but those were also the days when a depression was looming, and as the economy crumbled around them many record buyers simply retreated to their radios, where the music was free. Record sales quickly fell to one-fortieth of their level a decade earlier—at a time just after the purchase of radios had increased by well over 1,000 percent.

Radio, therefore, became the primary medium for country music, and few of the stations that chose to dabble in it were disappointed with their decision. One station that wandered into the field, almost timidly at first, but then with considerable gusto, was powerful WLS in Chicago. A year and a half before the birth of the Grand Ole Opry five hundred miles to the south, WLS had booked a fifteen-minute country show by a young, college-educated Kentucky guitarist named Bradley Kincaid. Kincaid's rollicking renditions of traditional mountain ballads drew what was rapidly becoming the typical audience response—dozens of calls and letters demanding an encore—and the WLS executives decided to launch their own barn-dance program similar to the pioneer show in Fort Worth. The program quickly caught on, and for more than a decade WLS was the most-listened-to country station anywhere in America.

It didn't take long, however, for the Grand Ole Opry to gain considerable respectability of its own. It received its name from a chance quip by its founder and master of ceremonies, George D. Hay, shortly after the program went on the air. Hay's broadcast followed NBC's "Musical Appreciation Hour," and tradition has it that one night early in 1926, the network show ended with a symphonic composition depicting the rush of a speeding locomotive. Hay, whether to make a point or simply to poke some fun, decided to open his program with DeFord Bailey, a popular harmonica soloist, and his arrangement of a driving and equally graphic train song called "Pan American Blues."

"For the past hour," Hay is reported to have said in introducing Bailey's number, "we have been listening to grand opera. But from now on we are going to hear the Grand Ole Opry"—which is what it has been ever since.

Virtuoso instrumental performances by people like Bailey, the Crook Brothers, the Fruit Jar Drinkers, and Fiddlin' Arthur Smith dominated the Opry in its early years. One of the few performers whose singing was as important as his picking was a zesty old banjoist named Uncle Dave Macon, who often performed with the able backup support of Sam and Kirk McGee. Macon had turned pro in 1918 when a farmer paid him fifteen dollars to play for a party, and his reputation had grown steadily between that time and his first appearance on the Opry in 1926.

Many of his songs were ballads he had picked up just before the turn of the century from laborers in the mines, railroad yards, and riverboat docks throughout the upper South. The tunes were almost invariably up-tempo and escapist, but the lyrics—especially in songs like "Buddy Won't You Roll Down the Line"—contained some undisguised social commentary on the effects of the Industrial Revolution on the workers of the South.

Macon died in 1953, and with his passing the Opry lost its most important link with the past. The subject matter and the sound of the music began to change, to lose at least a little of its edge, as vocal performances and backup instrumentation became more and more polished, and the formulas for commercial success became more and more apparent.

Lovesick singers had already begun to overshadow the other Opry acts, beginning with the arrival of Roy Acuff in 1939 and continuing over the next several decades with the appearance of sophisticated country crooners like Eddy Arnold and Jim Reeves. Uncle Dave Macon, however, was survived by a few of his early-day cronies, and a stubborn handful—

Herman Crook, Claude Lampley, and Sam and Kirk McGee—were still alive and picking when the Opry changed locations.

The oldest of the old-timers was Sam McGee, who in 1974 was living outside Nashville on a five-hundred-acre cattle and tobacco farm that he still worked himself. The road leading to it wound its way randomly around the steep Tennessee hillsides, constantly and casually doubling back on itself, until finally you arrived at a rust-spattered mailbox jammed into a milk can with the words "Sam F. McGee" hand-painted on top.

Inside the sturdy stone farmhouse the rooms were moderately cluttered with the trappings of his work—two guitars and a banjo stashed away in the living-room corners, an ASCAP silver service award "for over a half-century of constant and heart-rendering contributions" hung on the wall, and records strewn on the dining-room table. Next to the living-room fireplace was a smaller table with a Bethlehem manger scene permanently in place and an unframed, autographed picture of George Wallace leaning next to it.

On the day after the Opry left the Ryman, McGee leaned forward in his creaky old rocking chair and began to expound in his genial and self-effacing way on the changes he had seen. "It's just so different today," he said. "You have about fifty musicians for every one we had back then, but you know I honestly believe the music in those days was better. You had nothing but the pure sound. Now you have all sorts of drums and amplification and all that. I don't know, I may just have an old fogey attitude, but I do know I still get a lot of letters from people asking, 'Why can't we get more of the old style country music like you play?'"

"Back then, you didn't figure to go into music as a profession," McGee continued, warming to the subject, his clear eyes taking on a sparkle as the recollections came back. "No, in those days people just played for the love of music. During those first few shows, the solemn old judge [George Hay] couldn't pay us anything because the program wasn't making enough money. We didn't care. We loved the music and we knew he would do the best he could if the program survived."

By the time the Opry was doing well enough to spend forty-three million dollars on the new Opryland complex, its executives were paying McGee an average of thirty-six dollars a Saturday night, and so he still made his living, as he always had, from farming.

He generally played two slots on each Opry show—one as part of a group known as the Fruit Jar Drinkers, and the other in a featured performance with his brother, Kirk. The McGees often played their original compositions, and on Grand Opening Night at the new Opry house they chose a quintessential country song called "When the Wagon Was New"—which celebrates a simpler time when people were in less of a hurry and money was only a means to an end.

Sam and Kirk pioneered their own picking style, and among the more serious connoisseurs of musical talent it is the object of considerable awe. Most scholars agree that Sam McGee was one of the most influential guitarists in the history of country music, but a few people around the Opry will tell you that among the program's current executives, he and his brother were not exactly considered hot commercial property. That assessment showed in a variety of ways.

For example Sam McGee, who believed that many of his fans were old people and farmers, who preferred to go to bed early, had been pleading for years for an earlier slot on the Opry, but without any success. "I hope if I live to be old enough, I'll get it," he confided in 1974. "I think maybe I will, but we'll just have to see."

He didn't. With his request for an early spot still pending, he was killed in a tractor accident in 1975.

Two other old-timers, Ed Hyde and Staley Walton, died about the same time, and in a way their passing was even more revealing than McGee's. Hyde played fiddle, and Walton guitar, with a veteran group called the Crook Brothers. A few weeks after they died, the group's leader, seventy-six-year-old Herman Crook, went to Opry manager Hal Durham to tell him who he wanted as a replacement for Hyde.

"Well, he [Durham] told me they weren't sure if they were going to replace him or not," Crook remembered bitterly, a few months after the conversation. "I couldn't believe what I was hearing. I said, 'You mean you're not going to let me have my fiddle player?' Well, 'course I had to have a fiddle player, and eventually they did let me have the boy I wanted.

"But I never have gotten anybody to play the guitar. Only guitar player now is old Mr. [Bert] Hutchenson, and he's eighty-three. I reckon they're just kinda waiting for us to die off. Seems like, anyway.

"I don't want anybody to boost me up," he continued, talking backstage at the Opry, staring down at the rough wood floor. "I just want to be treated right. Right is right anywhere. It reminds me of a man raising up his children—and maybe they go against him, forget their parents. That's kinda how it's been.

"Fellows like us," he concluded, "oughta be right in there. We were the backbone of the Opry. I'm worried that when we go, our music will too."

It might. For country has always been an accurate reflection of the society around it, and that society has changed a lot since the glory days of Herman Crook and Sam McGee.

But there are two ways the music can reflect the society: It can mirror its mass-produced and synthetic qualities, or it can penetrate deeper, to the joys and anguish, the sorrows and peculiarities of the modern time. Country music today is doing both. There is a rebellious class of musicians around places like Nashville, Austin, and Bakersfield—a feisty, sometimes temperamental bunch, who write with poetic fervor about nearly every aspect of the human condition: war, peace, growing old, dying, loneliness, love, tolerance, prejudice.

By the midseventies the best of these entertainers—people like Waylon Jennings and Tom. T. Hall—had come to see the Opry as the classic victim of country music's very popularity: a big-business, multimillion-dollar enterprise, curiously incompatible with the music itself, which has always sprung from the hopes and failures of a far different class of people.

A striking example of the difference in perspective between Opry fans and Opry executives (which illuminates, in addition, two divergent strains in American conservatism: one of them folksy and unsystematic, the other corporate and close-to-the-vest) occurred just before Christmas of 1973. It centered on the unlikely person of Skeeter Davis, a wide-eyed, attractive blond and long-time Ryman regular, who produced some enormous hits in the early sixties. The effusive Miss Davis had been struck by the irony of the Nashville police having arrested a handful of local Jesus freaks who, in their starry-eyed seasonal zeal, had managed to aggravate a number of harried Christmas shoppers with persistent affirmations that Jesus loved them. When she performed on the night of December 8, Miss Davis told the applauding Opry faithful:

"I appreciate, and a while ago, I sang my record and everything. But we're having a great thing happening in Nashville—the Jesus people are here. They're having Jesus rallies every night out at Second and Lindsey Avenue. And a while ago—this is something I just feel like I should share it; I didn't ask our manager—but they've arrested fifteen people just for telling people that Jesus loves them. That really burdens my heart, so I thought I would come to the Opry tonight and sing. Here we are, celebrating Jesus's birthday. He's liable to come before Christmas, before Santa Claus does. That's something to think about. I would like to sing for y'all this song."

When she completed her reedy-voiced rendition of "Amazing Grace," the fans responded with warm, sustained applause. But once the show was over, Miss Davis was abruptly suspended from the cast for criticizing the police and infusing the Opry with unwanted political controversy.

Not long after the Skeeter Davis episode and the Opry's departure from the Ryman, the controversy grew even more intense when one of the program's best-known contemporary entertainers, singer and songwriter Tom T. Hall, withdrew from the cast. The immediate reason for his decision was a long-standing Opry rule prohibiting a full set of drums, but in an interview about six months after he left, Hall acknowledged that his reasons went deeper.

"As soon as we moved to the new place, I immediately and instinctively did not like it," he explained. "The Ryman was different. It was almost an ego trip, really, standing on the same stage where Hank Williams once performed, and knowing there were people out there who appreciated what you were doing, who had driven in some cases a couple hundred miles to see it.

"But the audiences now don't know what they are looking at. The old-time acts are being put down and dismissed. They're playing to people who don't know what they are seeing, who stop in at Opryland on their way to Florida, and take in a performance of the Opry and think, 'What the hell is this guy doing?'"

Hall offered his criticisms late in 1974, and he was certainly not alone in holding that position. By 1977, however, there were diverse signs that the

Opry's leaders, stung by the persistent bad press, had begun taking steps to repair the image. They had added to the cast such widely respected performers as Ronnie Milsap, one of the country music's top male vocalists throughout the mid-seventies, and Don Williams, a mellow-voiced Texan whose folky, low-key ballads have made him one of the most universally respected performers in country music.

There have also been guest performances by country-rock rebel Charlie Daniels, and others known for their musical innovations. And George Hamilton IV, whose close affiliation with the folk and protest singers of the sixties raised some eyebrows a decade ago, has rejoined the cast after an absence of several years. Says Hamilton, "I find much of the same spirit and enthusiasm that made the Opry such a great institution in the first place."

Hamilton is no Pollyanna. He knows that the Opry has had its problems, but like Hall, he believes the same commercializing pressures are at work in country music as a whole. Whether they will prevail remains to be seen, but in the meantime there are some outstanding pickers and poets who are striving—on behalf of themselves and their musical genre—not to be ruined by success. To understand the tension under which they labor, you have to go back about a quarter of a century, to the days when the Grand Ole Opry was at the peak of its popularity.

# 2

# THE TRADITION-MINDED REBELS: Hank Williams, Waylon Jennings, & Tompall Glaser

**Tell me one more time, just so's I'll understand
Are you sure Hank done it this way?***

—*Waylon Jennings*

On the morning of August 11, 1952, Hank Williams was lying in the back seat of a Cadillac outside of WSM, drunk, depressed, and, as of a few hours earlier, out of work. He had just been fired from the Grand Ole Opry, and although another job was waiting at the "Louisiana Hayride" in Shreveport, Hank felt all the consolation that a deposed chairman of the board would find in knowing he could still be head cashier. The Opry, in those days, was the top of the country music heap, and Hank had struggled long and hard to get there.

*©1975 by Baron Music Publishing Co. International Copyright Secured/All rights reserved. Used by permission of the copyright owner.

There are surprisingly *few* good photos of Hank Williams, but here the all-time master of sad country songs is caught in the frame of mind that gave poignance to his music. (Photo courtesy the Country Music Foundation Library.)

Mel Brown, glib-fingered lead guitarist for blues great Bobby Bland, moved to Nashville and hit the road in 1976 in Tompall Glaser's country band. (Photo by Charlyn Zlotnik, courtesy ABC Dot Records.)

Tompall Glaser, a serious, determined musician has been pursuing his own peculiar blend of blues and country. (Photo courtesy MGM Records.)

Once he had arrived, however, he had taken it by storm, beginning with his first guest shot on June 11, 1949. People who were there that night maintain with absolute conviction that it was one of the most exciting moments in the history of country music. Such assessments can't be measured, of course, but there is very little evidence to prove them wrong. Williams encored six or seven times, singing over and over again the song that brought him to the Opry in the first place, a Tin Pan Alley number called "Lovesick Blues."

It was Hank's first big hit, and in the hands of a lesser artist it might have been a mediocre song, filled as it was with uninspired couplets such as this one: "I've grown used to you somehow/I'm nobody's sugar daddy now." But when Hank would get to the chorus and let loose his yodeling moan about being lo-onesome, the people in the audience understood exactly what he meant, and the thunderous, foot-stomping ovations threatened to tear the tar paper right off the Ryman.

Hank projected that same kind of energy wherever he went, his six-foot, hundred-and-forty-pound frame taking on commanding and charismatic proportions as the applause reverberated through his head and lit up the grin on his high-boned face. At least that's how it was when he was sober. When he was drunk (and he stayed that way a good part of the time during the waning months of his life), he couldn't sing a lick, and half the time they would find him passed out in some hotel room, unable to appear at all.

When the cancellations became commonplace, the people at the Opry felt they had no choice but to drop him from the cast, and although Hank was determined until the end to make a triumphant return, he never did. He died, apparently from the accumulated effects of too much alcohol, a few hours into New Year's of 1953—passed out in his car, as he and a young driver were heading for a show date in Canton, Ohio. He was twenty-nine.

The brevity of Hank Williams's career has sparked continual speculations about how things might have been if he hadn't been driven to the bottle by whatever it was that drove him. The point is obviously moot, and his biographer, Roger M. Williams (no relation), speculates plausibly that Hank's drinking and his astonishing abilities as a songwriter may have sprung from the same inner agonies. Whatever it was that gave Williams his power of feeling, the songs that grew out of that power include some of the most impressive ever written, not only in country music, but in any other field as well. To this day, he is probably the most imitated singer and songwriter that country music has ever produced, and that fact has proved a double-edged sword. Hank wasn't a bad one to imitate, but slicked-up carbons seldom have the freshness of original versions, and country music has had to contend with that reality for the last twenty-five years.

At first glance, it seems a little strange that would be the case. As you read through the lyrics of a Hank Williams song, the words are so simple, so obvious—the vocabulary about what you would expect from a small-town Alabama boy who grew up during the Depression with an utter lack of interest in formal, or even informal, schooling. But if the songs themselves are uncomplicated, the emotions they captured are not, and that's what gives them the kind of gut-stabbing realism that country music fans have always remembered.

One of Williams's best-known songs, for example, is "Cold, Cold Heart," which, on the surface at least, seems almost trite. It is the lament of a lovesick hillbilly whose woman is still hung up on a man who done her wrong.

> **Another love before my time**
> **Made your heart sad and blue**
> **And so my heart is paying now**
> **For things I didn't do.***

Very uncomplicated. But as the verses unfold, it turns out that the singer is not simply trapped in a wallow of self-pity. He is also hurt by the woman's own unhappiness, which is genuine and multilayered. Part of it stems from the simple fact of having been wronged by another man, but also, the song suggests, from the knowledge that life is passing her by while she is trapped by a grief and a repression of feelings that she can't seem to control.

All in all, it's a subtle and true-to-life twist on the unrequited-love genre, and yet it's so simply done that you don't think through it to appreciate it, any more than Hank probably thought through it to write it. The communication is potent, instantaneous, with no special need for critical analysis.

The same is true, even more emphatically, of a song that many people believe is the best Hank ever wrote. It began as four scrawled lines on a scrap of paper, and at first he didn't know quite what to think of them. He took them to a songwriter friend named Jimmy Rule to ask if they made any sense. These were the lines:

> **Did you ever see a robin weep**
> **As leaves begin to die**
> **That means he's lost the will to live**
> **I'm so lonesome I could cry.** *

Rule assured him they made pretty good sense, and with a little coaching and polishing from his publisher, Fred Rose, Williams achieved a nearly perfect evocation of loneliness. "I'm So Lonesome I Could Cry" was a watershed song for country music—16 lines of metaphor and imagery that comprise not the straightforward story line of an old-fashioned ballad, or even Williams's usual description of a particular situation, but rather a haunting word picture of an abstract feeling.

> **Hear that lonesome whippoorwill**
> **He sounds too blue to fly**
> **The midnight train is whining low**
> **I'm so lonesome I could cry.**
>
> **I've never seen a night so long**
> **When time goes crawling by**
> **The moon just went behind a cloud**
> **To hide its face and cry.**
>
> **The silence of a falling star**
> **Lights up a purple sky**
> **And as I wonder where you are**
> **I'm so lonesome I could cry.** *

The quality of the poetic components varies a little from verse to verse. Certainly Hank didn't invent the concept of time at a crawl. But all of it works and, in the last verse especially, the technique is as sophisticated as any you'll find. The metaphor of a sky being lit by silence is precisely the way it strikes the brain—hearing and sight are at work simultaneously, blended at the moment of perception.

And there are the smaller things. The sky is purple instead of dark, black, or something more obvious, and there is the subjunctive verb in the final line—he *isn't* crying, but he *could*—which suggests a kind of strength and endurance that is all the more lonesome because the feeling is bottled inside.

All in all, not too bad for an Alabama hillbilly, and yet Hank's songs appeared so simple that a lot of people who should have known better were inspired to travel his road. And that, unfortunately, is the other side of the Hank Williams legacy. Several generations of country musicians have set about copying the twang and the tear in his hard-edged voice, and the unobtrusive technique of his gut-level songs. In many cases they have succeeded, or come pretty close, but in a larger sense of course they've failed. For imitation is the antithesis of creativity, and creativity was what the Hank Williams tradition was all about.

There are a few people around Nashville who have grabbed hold of that understanding, amid all the swirling debates about what's country music and what isn't, and whether anything can really be country in a suburban nation homogenized by prosperity and television. One of those people is Waylon Jennings, a tough but gentle west Texas good ole boy who cut his musical teeth as the bass player for Buddy Holly.

Jennings's rock 'n' roll background crops up from time to time in the beat of his music, but never in his voice, which has as much pure-grade country soul as any voice could have. He has become, in recent years, the most prominent of an ill-defined class of innovative musicians around Nashville—a rough-hewn, sometimes inarticulate bunch who are serious about their music and bristle at the still widely held assumption that if you don't sound a lot like Hank, you are somehow doing violence to the tradition of country music.

In his words and his actions, Jennings has refuted that notion. He has boycotted the Grand Ole Opry because they won't let him use a full set of drums, recorded songs by Bob Dylan and other noncountry writers, and made pioneer appearances at such big-city night spots as the Troubadour and Max's Kansas City.

And yet, for all of that, he is as much preoccupied with the roots of country music as any other performer. The fans instinctively understand that fact, and those who pour in for his concerts are not only the younger and shaggier believers who have rallied to the cause in recent years, but also the older, more crimson-necked fans—who, like the young, recognize Waylon as one of their own. And if there was ever any doubt in their minds, all they had to do was listen to his songs—his ode to Bob Wills, written on a plane between Dallas and Austin, and even more important, his Top Ten philosophical hit about the legacy of Hank. The latter tribute begins like this:

> **Lord, it's the same old tune,**
> **fiddle and guitar**
> **Where do we take it from here**
> **Rhinestone suits and new shiny cars**
> **It's been the same way for years**
> **We need a change***

Jennings performs that song nearly everywhere he goes these days, and on a recent swing through Atlanta he grabbed a few minutes backstage to talk about the thoughts behind it. "The key idea is expansion," he said. "That's what all of us are talking about. Hell, Hank just didn't live long enough. He'd be the most progressive guy around today. And Bob Wills was playing with a twenty-one-piece band, with horns and all that stuff—back in the forties, man. So the music keeps expanding. You look at any of the giants—Jimmie Rodgers, Bob Wills, Hank Williams—they all understood that, and all of us oughta be understanding it today."

The problem, in Jennings's view, is that the powers that be in Nashville have a history of timidity about change or expansion beyond a polishing of yesterday's rough edges. Frustration over such closed-mindedness became an obsession with Jennings, and eventually he banded together with a fellow nonconformist named Tompall Glaser to do battle with record company execs in the cause of greater independence.

To everyone's amazement, their efforts paid off. "About two years ago [in1974 ], I got the absolute musical freedom to do whatever I want," says Waylon, and so far the commercial results have been spectacular. Record sales are booming, his concerts are packed, and he was named country music's top male vocalist in 1975.

It remains to be seen how well Waylon, Glaser and all their buddies will cope with success. Waylon, in particular, has seemed a trifle bewildered by the uncritical admiration that has come his way, and the hard and fast living it has helped thrust upon him. It has unleashed some of the vagaries of his volatile personality—a darker, moody streak that coexists stubbornly with his fundamental decency.

He and Glaser had a falling-out in 1976, and wound up wrangling through lawyers about how to dissolve their business liaisons. But musically, all that is beside the point. Jennings et al. continue to embody a well-rooted willingness to change that keeps country music from going stale.

Nobody embodies that willingness more thoroughly than Glaser. Even though he is still a lesser phenomenon than Jennings is at this writing, he has struck out on the most unusual and radically creative direction of all. He has decided to fuse the sound of the the blues with the sound of country, which is not in itself unique. What is unique is that Glaser has approached the task in the most obvious possible way—by putting together a band that consists of both blues and country musicians. The idea jelled several years back when he wandered into the New York club Max's Kansas City to catch the closing act of a high-powered rhythm and blues singer by the name of Bobby Blue Bland.

Anchoring the band that night was lead guitarist Mel Brown, a native of Jackson, Mississippi, who had grown up on a steady diet of delta blues and had retained his affinity and fascination with the roots of Southern music. Glaser was stunned by the skill of Brown's picking, and after the show he called him aside, told him what he had in mind, and asked if he would be interested in coming to work in Nashville. Intrigued, Brown agreed to think it over, and about two years later he called Glaser to say he was ready. He brought with him drummer Charles Polk, another Mississippian, and together with Glaser and three top Nashville pickers, they embarked upon the task with an idealistic fervor.

"It just made good sense," explained Mel Brown before a recent show. "The roots, you know, are the same—hard times are on both sides. It's just that he [Glaser] is the only cat with enough nerve to do it this way. 'Stead of a white cat playing the blues licks, he has me and Charles."

By the spring of 1976, the blend had evolved well enough to go public with a new album and a major national tour. Reviewers, even in the highbrow *New York Times*, were ecstatic, and the crowds became downright unruly as they cheered and clapped and clamored for more. The scenes may not have rivaled, say, the Hank Williams debut at the Grand Ole Opry, but in places like Atlanta, Norfolk, and Chicago there were the same ripples of excitement as the fans realized they were hearing something fresh, different, and yet identifiably country.

One crucial test was Atlanta. The crowd that balmy mid-March night consisted entirely of the hard-core faithful, undiluted by the sprinkling of college kids and other young people who would turn out in other cities along the way. Mel Brown was vaguely uneasy, realizing that the time was not long past when such an assemblage might have waxed nasty at the sight of a couple of bear-sized black men playing the blues in a hillbilly band.

But on this particular night, the mood was friendly. The applause built steadily as Tompall opened the show with a Tom Paxton folk song called "The Last Thing On My Mind," ran through a couple of straight country numbers, and then moved from center stage to let the band members do an instrumental and display their talents. The showstealer was Brown, bending over his guitar in rapt concentration and sending out a series of intricate, quick-fingered blues runs that drew half a dozen rounds of applause even before the song was finished.

Glaser lounged to one side, grinning, his elbow propped on an amplifier, and then moved back to the stage and broke into the old Jimmie Rodgers song, "T for Texas, T for Tennessee." There was symbolic significance in the choice, for Rodgers is legendary for his own peculiar blending of country and blues—his 12-bar stanzas, repeated lines, and guitar runs borrowed from the black railroad workers he had known in Mississippi.

In his early teens, Rodgers had landed a job carrying water to the depot workers in Meridian, and he was inevitably there during break time, when they retreated to their banjos and guitars. He learned to play both instruments during those years, and he also learned songs and fragments of songs that he would use later on in his recording career.

Because of recurring bouts with tuberculosis, Rodgers left railroad work after fourteen years, determined to make it as a professional musician. After knocking around for a couple of years, he landed a job in 1927 singing blues and mountain ballads at radio station WWNC in Asheville, North Carolina. In July of 1927, he learned that Ralph Peer, then of Victor Records, would soon be in the nearby town of Bristol, Tennessee, monitoring recording sessions for aspiring hillbilly singers.

Rodgers hustled over, got recorded, and when his music became moderately popular over the next few months, the Victor people decided that they had signed a potential star. They brought him to the company studios in Camden, New Jersey, for more extensive recording sessions, and it was on the first session that Rodgers cut "T for Texas, T for Tennessee." The song proved to be significant for him in a number of ways. It was a hit, for one thing. But, more important in the long run, it also marked the first time that he used his patented "blue yodel"—a homespun bit of vocal gymnastics in which he allowed his voice to warble from octave to octave, producing the pained and lonesome sound that was to become his trademark.

Tompall Glaser, whose whiskey baritone is not well suited to yodeling, doesn't sing the song in quite the same way. But the fact that he does it at all underscores what he regards as a deeper kinship between himself, Rodgers, and some of the other unorthodox musicians who have come along from time to time in the history of country music.

The liner notes of his first album in 1976 sum it up very well. "Tompall does not break down tradition when he brings a new idea or arrangement to the studio or stage," the notes affirm. "He does not break down tradition any more than Jimmie Rodgers did with his blues, Hawaiian instruments or use of Louis Armstrong on sessions. Or any more than Ernest Tubb did with his electric guitar or Hank Williams with a sound that changed all music or Johnny Cash with his protest songs or Waylon Jennings with his rock beat. There may be a break from traditional form of expression, but there is no break from the tradition of looking ahead and trying new ideas."

"Hell," agrees Tompall, "what we're doing's not radical. We're just going after the entire spectrum of our roots, and the roots of country and the roots of blues are the same. It's going to be fun to live it and put it together."

That view of country music has become common around Nashville in the last couple of years—the assumption that the Nashville sound is closely related to a number of other musical traditions, including blues, rock, and even the folk-protest sounds of Pete Seeger and Woody Guthrie. That assumption has always been around, but it had become submerged beneath the rhetoric and the reality of all the political and social forces that were affecting country music between the mid-fifties and the early seventies.

The rediscovery of common ground has become a pivotal motif in country music in the seventies, and, as much as anything else, it is responsible for the renewed power and the broadened appeal of the country tradition. The thing that ties Roy Acuff to Willie Nelson, or Tompall Glaser to Charlie Daniels, or Kitty Wells to Emmylou Harris, is that they are all concerned in one way or another with getting back to the roots.

# 3

# THE ESTRANGEMENT OF COUNTRY & FOLK:
## Losing Sight of the Common Ground

**He's a poor man 'cause mining's all he's known
and miners don't get rich loading coal©**

*—Hazel Dickens*

The roots. They run deep into the life-style of places like Clark County, Kentucky, an ancient aggregation of coal-country foothills and rolling bluegrass farmlands. In the western reaches of the county, perched on a hilltop overlooking the Kentucky River, is the pale green cabin of Asa Martin. He built it himself in the early sixties and, for a few years at least, it served as the haven he intended—a secluded home base for some serious bass fishing down on the river, and maybe a little neighborly guitar-picking later in the evening.

Eventually, however, they found him. Some professors from the West Coast stumbled upon the fact that he was still alive, and they reacted with

A hand-crafted mandolin hangs on the wall of an Appalachian farmhouse. Scholars who came to the mountains were stunned to discover that nearly everybody made some kind of music. (Photo by Douglas Green.)

The mountains were never a region of plenty, but there was a dignity about life within sturdy wooden cabins, and it spilled over into the music. (Photo by Steve Perille.)

Opposite:   When mountain music became intertwined with the issues of poverty and exploitation that affected the region, it became the ancestor for American protest music as well as commercial country music. (Photo courtesy *The Charlotte Observer*.)

Change came slowly to the hillsides and hollows. For years they were a place where the old British folk ballads could evolve quietly into something distinctively American. (Photo by Dot Jackson.)

all the gleeful disbelief of prospectors in the presence of a fist-sized nugget. The professors were writing the story of old-time, country-folks music, and Asa Martin has been a part of that story off and on for the last fifty years— ever since the mid-twenties when he and Fiddlin' Doc Roberts met in a Winchester barbershop, got to talking and picking, and decided on the spot to put together a band.

That decision soon led them to the "WLS Barn Dance" in Chicago, to shows of their own at WHAS in Louisville and WLW in Cincinnati, and finally to the Grand Ole Opry in Nashville. In between, Asa recorded more than six hundred record sides and wrote some enormously popular songs, including "Hot Corn, Cold Corn," made famous by Flatt and Scruggs, and "I'm Going Back to Alabam'," recorded by everybody from Martin himself to Pat Boone.

Asa is recording again today. The music is in his blood, and at age seventy-five, he has the look of a man who is happy with his life. His frame has become a trifle gaunt and bent with age, but his sun-tanned face— uncrinkled except around the eyes and the smile—exudes the serenity you find among old people who have spent their years well, and know it.

As Asa settles back into his lived-in easy chair and begins to reminisce, the memories are still sharp and he will pull out the tattered old scrapbook with the yellowing handbills and newspaper clippings, the promotional fliers with the dates and titles of his records. "Here's an old one," he says, fumbling with a flier dated January 15, 1930, and affirming that among the latest batch of Gennett Records was "Down on the Farm" by Asa Martin.

The song, which Asa will sing for you with a quick a cappella approximation of the original version, tells the story of a young man returning to the old home place, where the memories flood his brain and a stranger greets him at the door. "I learned that from Mama," he said. "Back around 1904, I guess it was. She used to sing it around the kitchen. Music was a big pastime back then—that was before it went commercial, and it played a big part in people's lives."

That fact was impressed upon people like Ralph Peer, who came South in the twenties to record the Appalachian musicians, and Cecil Sharp, the English musicologist who traveled to the mountains a few years before Peer in search of old British folk ballads that had survived in the New

World. He found them all right, but he found a few other things that he had not been expecting.

One of those things, he later explained, was the bearing of the people— a kind of sturdiness and self-containment coexisting with the poverty and isolation; a sharp contrast, he concluded, to the shuffling obsequiousness of many British peasants. But the most striking thing was more simple and more directly related to his musical mission: It was the fact that everybody made music; everybody.

Sharp and others have concluded from that fact that music in the mountains served a far more crucial function than simple entertainment. "It was," says Loyal Jones, an ardent folklorist at Berea College in Kentucky, "the literature of the people. Just as the ballads had been an important form of literature in the British Isles, they also served a similar function here."

In addition, the late Buell Kazee, a preacher and legendary banjo picker who cut fifty-six record sides back in the twenties, maintained that in the days before psychoanalysis and all the other sanity-preserving sciences and pseudosciences of the present, music was a way of preserving equilibrium.

Asa Martin agrees. He remembers boyhood hikes down the narrow, tree-choked hollow just south of Winchester, when he and his family would lug along their guitars, and the neighbors would do the same. They would all rendezvous at a little weatherbeaten church, sparsely equipped with poplar-bench pews, and they would sing for hours—religious songs mostly, but others as well: fiddle tunes and Old World ballads, and also the indigenous compositions of tragedy and hard times.

There was an entirely different feel at such gatherings from the mood today at the dozens of old-time music festivals that are beginning to crop up throughout the South. When a quarter of a million pot-smoking, bare-breasted, stringy-haired young people will descend upon the hamlet of Union Grove, North Carolina, to revel in the music of mountain-grown fiddlers, it is obvious right off the bat that something is different.

It's true that on the surface what's going on appears to be a remarkable resurgence of tradition, a modern communion with the spirit of the past. But in a fundamental sense, it isn't. And the difference is not simply the age, appearance, and life-style of the fans, but rather their relationship with the music. For example, when Doc Watson, the virtuoso guitar-picking native of Deep Gap, North Carolina, came down from the hills for a recent bluegrass festival in Charlotte, he found himself confronted by thousands of wildly appreciative people—but they were so appreciative that their adrenalin levels were a little on the abnormal side, and they swarmed toward the stage, shrieking and clapping and obliterating the lyrics and the musical subtleties that are, in Watson's view, what the music is all about.

"Hey," he told them in tones that were at once genial and sternly disapproving, "if you're not gon' listen, I'm not gon' pick. I mean that thing."

The fans were genuinely bewildered, for throughout the evening, until Watson's appearance, they had simply responded like typical bluegrass fanatics—stomping in time with the showy fiddle and banjo runs that are intended to produce precisely that kind of frantic response. But the older-vintage musicians like Watson, Asa Martin, and Buell Kazee see a big difference between their craft and modern-day bluegrass. They may like bluegrass, may appreciate the talent that goes into its production, but they are aware of a crucial and subtle distinction between it and the tradition out of which it grew.

Bluegrass is pure entertainment, evolving during the last several decades through the consummate skills of people like Earl Scruggs, Lester Flatt, and Bill Monroe. It sounds, in many respects, very similar to its predecessor. Both rely chiefly on a blend of banjos, fiddles, and guitars; and in addition, the old-time music had its share of fast-paced reels and hoedown numbers—aimed, like bluegrass, at producing the same sort of rollicking retreat from reality. But bluegrass has a different spirit, a much greater emphasis on individual showmanship, that is at odds, somehow, with the natural modesty that runs through the mountain character.

And there is also a difference in the type of emotion expressed by each musical form, and therefore in its ultimate, overriding purpose. Today's bluegrass is almost never sad, while yesterday's mountain music often was. When Asa Martin, for example, looks back on the evenings at the rugged old church, the things that stand out in his mind are the slow and ballady songs like "Railroad Boy," a New World rewrite of an old English standard, which tells the story of a mournful young girl committing suicide in the cause of unrequited love. There were also, Martin remembers, the purely localized compositions—songs like "The Death of Edward Hawkins," the autobiography of a young Kentucky man who was hanged for murder at the age of twenty-three and who, according to legend, sang his confessions from the scaffold moments before the rope snapped taut.

"There were a lot of songs about sadness and tragedy," Martin remembers with a somber nod of his head. "Don't know quite why that was, really, 'cept it just seems natural when things go wrong, when tragedies hit, that you would make up a song about it."

And that, above all else, has been the distinguishing feature of mountain music throughout the years. Its primary purpose lies less in escape and entertainment than in a head-on coping with whatever the world can throw at you.

Given that fact, it was not surprising that the music of Appalachia would soon become intertwined with the social and political issues that had begun to prevail. In the very early days of the Grand Ole Opry, Uncle Dave Macon raised a few eyebrows with a hard-hitting song called "Buddy, Won't You Roll Down the Line"—protesting, among other things, the coal company bosses' using convict labor to drive down the wages of working people. There were a fair number of songs like it, for there was a lot to protest in the mountains of the South.

Most people who have never been there think of Appalachia as a remote and backward place, devoid of good roads and modern methods of communication—the kind of place where the folk songs of England could endure for centuries with very little change. And for centuries that view was pretty much correct. But in the past several decades the pace of change has been astounding, particularly so to the people who have lived through it. Roads and television have made the mountains accessible to outside influences, and the accessibility has proved a mixed blessing at best.

The coal companies, for example, claim to have created jobs, and no doubt they have. But they have also transformed much of Appalachia from a subsistence-farming area into one of the most industrialized parts of the country, outside the big cities of the north.

Such industrial revolutions, of course, have never been very pretty, and when the companies arrived in the mountains, the by-products of their coming were depressingly similar to conditions in Europe a century or so earlier. Nimrod Workman, a skinny and toothless ex-miner and blues singer from West Virginia, remembers the days during Woodrow Wilson's administration when he would enter the mines so early, and emerge so late, that he seldom saw the sun. For that, he says, he and his comrades were paid $2.80 a day—generally in scrip that was redeemable only at company-owned stores. In the evening they would wander home to the tiny cabins that they rented for six dollars a month, coming in so exhausted that "there wasn't much to do but sing a little bit and go to bed."

Coal camp songs thus became a desperately popular tradition in the mountains, a last-ditch bastion of sanity and perspective that helped sustain the people who were forced to create them. Among the most famous of the mining songs, particularly in the outside world, were "Sixteen Tons" and "Dark As a Dungeon," both of them written by Merle Travis, a guitar-picking native of western Kentucky who escaped the mines through the skill in his fingers.

"Dark As a Dungeon," recorded by everybody from Chad Mitchell to Grandpa Jones, is the better song of the two, and it was written, oddly enough, when Travis was 3,000 miles away from the mines. "I was driving home after a date with a beautiful girl in Redondo Beach, California," he explained to writer Dorothy Horstman. "I had a recording session to do the next morning and needed some material. I parked my car under a street light and wrote the verses. Sometimes the saddest songs are written when a person is happy."

Not always, however. There were dozens of mountain writers who were never able to escape, and whose songs were as sad as any you'll find. They may not have had Travis's great skill with words, but they did have their own style of rough-edged eloquence that comes when you really have to live it. One of the best of these writers was a handsome, strong-faced woman balladeer by the name of Hazel Dickens. She had seen her share of Appalachian tragedy, and this, in part, was how she responded to it:

He's a poor man 'cause mining's all he's known
And miners don't get rich loading coal

He's a sick man 'cause that coal dust took its stand
But he don't expect to get no help from that operator man.
   Well it's good-bye Old Timer, I guess our time has come
   Those water holes, that dirty coal dust eating up our lungs
   We'll leave this world just as poor as the day we saw the sun
   Well it's good-bye Old Timer, all our mining is done.
I remember the time when I could load more coal than any man
Now my health is gone, buried down in that dirty ground
And they've taken away my rights, privilege to be a man
But I know I can't tell all that to the operator man.©

There's a rough and angry quality to the sadness, and it's appropriate for a line of work as dangerous as hammering for coal a mile inside a mountain. But it's a peculiar kind of anger—very fatalistic. In the polished million-sellers of Merle Travis, as well as in the down-home coal camp blues of Hazel Dickens or Nimrod Workman, the affirmation of humanity lies not in overcoming, but in staring the son-of-a-bitch right in the face and taking whatever it has to offer.

For many years, that point of view was prevalent in the mountains, but as every generation learns and relearns, the fatalism of the father eventually gives way to the anger of the son; and by the early sixties, Appalachian writers such as Billy Edd Wheeler were turning out lyrics such as these:

I've never been one to walk in lines,
Picket with placards, or carry signs.
But maybe I'm behind the times.©

Those three lines are the bridge in "They Can't Put It Back," a song Wheeler wrote more than fifteen years ago when he was returning for a visit to his grandfather in the West Virginia mountains of his boyhood. Things had changed a lot since his departure for Warren Wilson College in North Carolina, then Berea, then Yale, and finally the beginnings of a songwriting career in New York City. He was aghast at what he saw on the trip back home.

"I was driving along Big Coal River, on one of those little old mountain roads," he remembers, "and I came to a spot where they had been strip-mining. The machines had literally taken off the top of a mountain, and the debris was scattered down the hillsides. I had a very emotional reaction to that—I had also flown over the area and seen what they were doing in a lot of West Virginia and Kentucky. So I sat down and wrote something a little bit different—straight, hard protest."

Wheeler has been best known over the years for a different type of song—the novelty numbers like his own country hit, "Ode To The Little Brown Shack Out Back," or the Kingston Trio's "Reverend Mr. Black," or the torrid love song "Jackson," made popular by Johnny and June Carter Cash (and later by Nancy Sinatra and Lee Hazlewood). But after his move to New York City, and some initial coaching by pop writers Jerry Lieber and Mike Stoller, Wheeler fell in very compatibly with some of the protest singers of Greenwich Village.

Judy Collins, among others, would periodically wander over to his dumpy apartment in Brooklyn and listen by the hour to tapes of his songs, for she had always been known as one of the most meticulous of the folkies in her search for material. Eventually she recorded four Wheeler originals, and they chronicle in a poignant way the agonies and particularities of life in the mountains.

Perhaps the most haunting of them is "The Coming of the Roads," which, like most of Wheeler's compositions, is couched in human rather than ideological terms. But its message is, if anything, more obvious and rending than much of the straightforward protest that began to proliferate in the sixties. The song tells the story of a love affair gone sour, but it weaves the sadness through all the issues confronting Appalachia—the coming of the roads that made it accessible to outsiders, the rape of the land by the strip-mining machines, the weakening of values by the hunger for wealth. The woman in the song has been seduced by the new alien ways, and her lover offers his lament.

> We used to hunt the cool caverns
> Deep in our forest of green
> Then came the road and the taverns
> And you found a new love it seems
> Once I had you and the wildwood
> Now it's just dusty roads
> And I can't help from blaming your going
> On the coming
> The coming of the roads.©

There was an explosion of such songs in the late sixties and early seventies, and there was a great deal of talk about an emerging genre of mountain protest. This thinking was true as far as it went, but most of it contained at least one major flaw. It assumed that the modern explosion was something brand-new, and it wasn't. There was one brief period, more than forty years ago, when Depression-era radicalism combined with indigenous mountain conservatism to produce an extremely significant development in music. It was an instant, frozen in time, whose impassioned music was a progenitor not only of recent vintage country music, but of the Pete Seeger-Bob Dylan brand of protest music as well.

Some of the key figures during the period included Aunt Molly Jackson, Jim Garland, and Sarah Ogan Gunning, who were actually all members of the same family. Their father was Oliver Perry Garland, a young minister and coalminer who had been raised as a frontier farmer and then turned to the mines as Appalachian life began to change. He cast his lot with the unions at their very beginning, but change did not come overnight, and the family moved from one dingy coal camp to another in search of a more adequate living.

Like most miners in southeastern Kentucky, they never really found it, and throughout the area the sense of desperation began to grow. About the time the Great Depression descended on the country as a whole, conditions in the mines were reaching rock-bottom. The United Mine Workers union had fizzled in the face of stiff opposition, and in the area around Harlan County, Kentucky, the miners were ready when the tougher and more committed radicals of the Communist-backed National Miners Union arrived on the scene.

Even in retrospect, it was a peculiar mix: the determined New York radicals mingling with the intensely conservative coal camp people—the one group tracing its values and ideology to Karl Marx, the other to Daniel Boone and Jesus. The compatibility lay in the remnants of a frontier spirit, a sort of don't-tread-on-me independence that had long been a staple of Appalachian values—and also in the introduction by the union of an entirely new concept: hope. The idea of perfectibility, of radical alterations of the earthly condition, had never been a part of the mountaineers' experience. Times had generally been hard, and the quest, therefore, was for endurance and dignity in the face of the world's limited offerings.

But in the coal fields the times hit bottom, dignity came hard if at all, and in those circumstances, a strong radicalism began to take form in people such as Aunt Molly Jackson. Aunt Molly was a balladeer and a midwife. She had helped deliver more than a hundred miners' babies, only to watch helplessly as all too many of them died of malnutrition and childhood disease.

Two of those who died belonged to her half-sister, Sarah Ogan, whose husband also died of TB when the coal dust of the mines got the better of his lungs. In the early and mid-thirties, the two women—along with their brother, Jim Garland—began writing songs that chronicled the struggles of the union. Garland, for example, wrote "The Ballad of Harry Simms," a teenaged organizer who was gunned down in eastern Kentucky as he walked along a railroad track. (Garland's account does not mention the fact that a few weeks later, the coal company gun-thugs suspected of the killing were found slaughtered in exactly the same spot.)

Of all the writings of the day, however, none were any more revealing than those of Sarah Ogan (who later remarried, to become Sarah Gunning). Sarah, whose voice and compositions were recently recorded for preservation on Folk-Legacy Records, continued to sing all the old hymns and traditional numbers. But she also took the tunes to some of her favorites, including "Precious Memories," and transformed the lyrics into an amalgam of deeply personal lamentation and highly polemical exhortation in the cause of unionism.

She sang it all in a clear and mournful voice, rich in a hillbilly twang.

Dreadful memories, how they linger
How they ever flood my soul,
How the workers and their children
Die from hunger and from cold.

Hungry fathers, wearied mothers
Living in those dreadful shacks,
Little children cold and hungry
With no clothing on their backs.

Dreadful gun-thugs and stool-pigeons
Always flock around our door.
What's the crime that we've committed?
Nothing, only that we're poor.©

In the short run, such songs played an important role in the organizing process, but neither they nor the National Miners Union became a permanent force in the history of the mountains. The bitter thrust of coal-field radicalism was blunted by several factors—the reform and renewal of the more moderate United Mine Workers union, the New Deal with its aura of concern for the working man's plight, and finally, World War II.

The war, even more than Roosevelt's anti-Depression strategies, pumped life into the American economy, and certainly into American patriotism. The growing sense of fear and anger in the face of hard times became submerged beneath the national will to survive. And when radicalism re-emerged in the fifties and sixties, the music of protest was channeled in new directions—into the struggle against the out-front racism of the Deep South, the more subtly ingrained varieties farther north, and then against the new and peculiar war in Southeast Asia.

But the anthems of Sarah Ogan and Aunt Molly Jackson were more than a forgotten aberration. There was a direct and personal link between them and the music that was soon to come—a link that was forged between 1935 and the early forties, when the two sisters traveled to New York, singing their songs and seeking to drum up support for the battles in the coal camps. While they were there, they met and became friends with the godfathers of modern protest, a young and highly educated banjo player named Pete Seeger, and the hard-living poet of the Oklahoma dust bowl country, Woody Guthrie.

Both men were captivated by the utter simplicity of the women's commitment, and Seeger, especially, became a student of the folk music tradition of the southern mountains. His interest was more than political. He traveled south to study the picking style of Aunt Samantha Bumgarner, a versatile banjo and fiddle player from western North Carolina, and also of Bascom Lamar Lunsford, a legendary old banjo man from outside of Asheville whose right-wingish politics were enough to curl Seeger's hair.

Among all but the most hard-hit Southerners (as well as the industrial workers of the North), there was a tendency toward such politics in the years that followed the Depression. There had long been a natural conservatism in the region, a discomfort in the face of rapid change, and there were some uglier and murkier characteristics that would rear their heads from time to time—a sullen defensiveness dating back to the Civil War and Reconstruction, and a deeply embedded theology of racism that went back even further.

Even without all that, it was hard for white workers who had struggled their way through the viciousness of the thirties to comprehend the argument when blacks began to maintain that the game was rigged. After all, the white folks countered, they themselves had known hard times, but had worked and scrimped and persevered, and in the end it had all paid off. They had begun to sniff prosperity, and it was hard to acknowledge that something other than their own sweat and blood had made it all possible.

But, of course, something else had. The Depression went away when the war came along to prime the pump. But the depression surrounding black people did not go away, for it was a fixture of the system, carefully enforced, and condemning all but a few remarkable blacks to a second-class life and livelihood.

The idealism of the struggle against that system caught the imagination of Pete Seeger and the younger musicians that followed him—Bob Dylan, Joan Baez, Peter, Paul and Mary, Phil Ochs, and all the rest. But among the traditional fans of hillbilly music—the people who would retreat to their radios with the Grand Ole Opry, or besiege the Ryman on drizzly weekend evenings—the threat of new upheavals was the last thing they wanted to contemplate. The Protestant Ethic was reaping some rewards in the here-and-now, and there was an intolerance that soon bordered on outright hatred for those who would tear at the fabric that seemed to make those rewards possible.

The split between the fans of Pete Seeger and of, say, Roy Acuff was soon very striking, and the idea that the two forms of music had evolved directly—and over a remarkably short space of time—from the same point of origin began to seem wildly implausible.

But it didn't seem that way to everybody. There were people like Bobby Bare, a transplanted Ohio farm boy who would apply his rich and rustic baritone to offerings from both sides of the musical chasm. In the early sixties, soon after his arrival in Nashville, Bare recorded a song called "Detroit City," the story of a man who hops a north-bound freight looking for work and maybe a little bit of excitement, winds up with nothing but an assembly-line job and a drinking problem, and begins to yearn for the home and the girl he left down South.

The song was written by Danny Dill and Mel Tillis, a pair of Nashville-based writers whose hard-country credentials are absolutely impeccable. Tillis especially has a cornpone image—a stuttering central Floridian, tall and gaunt, he eventually made it big as a singer of straight country love songs.

About the same time that Bare came out with Tillis's song, he cut another record with a similar story . . . a restless young man is getting ready to cut loose for greener pastures, wrestling with the prospect of leaving his lover, but knowing that he will go and she will stay and neither of them will be very happy about it. The song was called "Four Strong Winds," and it was written by a Canadian singer named Ian Tyson.

Tyson at the time was half of the folk-singing duo of Ian and Sylvia, and in the minds of the fans at least he was identified strongly with the Peter, Paul and Mary branch of contemporary folk music. For one thing, he had the same manager (Albert Grossman), and so did Bob Dylan, Gordon Lightfoot, and a host of others.

But there was a similarity between Tyson's song and that of Mel Tillis, a sort of instinctive grasp of the same universal, that drew the attention of Bobby Bare and his producer, Chet Atkins. And as it turned out, the similarity was really no accident, for Tyson had grown up as country as Tillis, if not more so.

A decade and a half before all the cosmic cowboys crowded onto the scene in Nashville and in Austin, Texas, Tyson was appearing onstage in faded Levis and battered cowboy boots, and it all came naturally to him. He was raised in the cattle ranges of British Columbia and Alberta, listening to the same kind of music as his American country-boy contemporaries—the songs of Merle Travis, Flatt and Scruggs, the Carter Family, and also the spangled Canadian country stars like Hank Snow and Wilf Carter.

Eventually, Tyson and his guitar found themselves in Toronto, where he ran into an Ontario ballad singer named Sylvia Fricker. They decided to team up about the same time that the folk-music revival was rippling out from Newport and Greenwich Village, engulfing nearly everyone with a guitar and a desire to sing songs with a little bit of substance. But Tyson saw no contradiction between what he was singing and what he had always listened to, believing that all of it sprang from the same earthy source.

The same point of view was emphatically shared by his friend and fellow Canadian, Gordon Lightfoot, who would soon emerge as one of the biggest stars his country had ever produced, another pivotal figure in the reunification of folk and country music.

Lightfoot was a farm boy from outside the town of Orelia, Ontario. He had been raised on a radio diet of the Grand Ole Opry and the "Wheeling Jamboree," beaming his way from WSM in Nashville and WWVA in Wheeling, West Virginia. But then one day, as he later explained to his friends, he heard a Bob Dylan song called "Girl From the North Country," and he was bowled over by the craftsmanship of the lyrics. He decided on the spot to make a serious pursuit of songwriting, and the result was a steady outpouring of songs like "Early Morning Rain"—a blend of craftsmanship and earthiness that attracted the attention not only of Ian and Sylvia, and Peter, Paul and Mary, but also of a Grand Ole Opry singer named George Hamilton IV.

Hamilton has never been what you would call a country music purist. He began his recording career in 1956 with a million-selling rockabilly number called "A Rose and a Baby Ruth," and for the next several years he continued to churn out the teenybopper tearjerkers. But his private tastes were considerably more sophisticated, and in the early sixties he decided—long before it was a proved path to success—to pack up his family and move to Nashville.

According to nearly everybody who knows him, Hamilton is one of the most remarkable people ever to come through the city. He is tall and quiet, with unobtrusive good looks that are more wholesome than handsome. He sings pretty well, though there are scores of singers whose styles are more memorable; and yet somehow he has managed to hang on as a considerable force in the music business for the last twenty-one years.

The reason is deceptively simple. Hamilton is, as it happens, one of the most thoughtful people in country music, and one of the things he thinks about most often is the music itself—where it comes from, where it's all going, and all the other philosophical questions that make it more than just a pastime or a way to make a living. When he began to apply those tendencies to the music of the Canadian folkies, he soon realized that the songs they were doing were only a short step farther down a path on which he was already headed.

He didn't see much difference, for example, between "Early Morning Rain" and the "get-drunk-and-ramble" songs of Jimmie Rodgers. And certainly there was a similarity between Lightfoot's music and a song like "Abilene," which Hamilton had recorded in 1963. So he began to cut the songs of Lightfoot, Leonard Cohen, and Joni Mitchell, and they proved as successful as anything he had tried to date. Some of his Nashville picker-friends were dumbfounded.

"But the folkies and the Nashville pickers were operating out of the same heritage whether they wanted to acknowledge it or not," Hamilton says, looking back on the sixties. "There was a political split in those days. It was serious, but it was based on a set of conditions that appeared and have now begun to change. The common ground, I think, was much deeper."

Hamilton believes that the Canadians such as Lightfoot and Ian Tyson played a pivotal role in the rediscovery of that common ground, for there was, he says, a crucial distinction between them and their American counterparts. "Dylan and Joan Baez and the other Americans in the sixties folk revival were all highly political," Hamilton explains. "They perceived some major wrongs in the country, and it led them into folk protest.

"But in Canada, you had a generation of kids who grew up very differently. They were in a much bigger country, with only twenty million people. It was less crowded, and there was no war and no civil rights problem—at least not of the proportions that we had in this country. So when those Canadian young people began to write from their own experiences, they produced poetic, romantic, introspective lyrics, but not angry lyrics. And that was the major contribution of the Canadian folkies in bridging the gap to country music. It was easier to relate to what they were doing, because they were writing straight people-music, without the political overtones."

Hamilton believes that in the last ten years or so the gap has been bridged almost entirely. From the mid-sixties on, he and a host of others (Bobby Bare, Johnny Cash, Waylon Jennings, and Kitty Wells, to name a few) began recording the songs of Lightfoot, Tyson, and even Bob Dylan. The folkies themselves soon caught the spirit and began streaming through Nashville to record their albums, or to appear on Johnny Cash's show on ABC, or simply to hang out in the motels and bars and trade some songs.

It was, Hamilton and others maintain, a watershed era in the recent history of American music. For one thing, it helped make possible the emergence of a whole new generation of songwriters—Kris Kristofferson, Mickey Newbury, Dick Feller, John Hartford, Guy Clark, and dozens more—who have combined the lyrical finesse of the folkies with the gritty simplicity of Hank Williams.

But there was even more to the reunion than that. It was a metaphor—a prelude—to a national depolarization. For when Bob Dylan and Johnny Cash begin issuing formal declarations of soulbrotherhood, and Joan Baez begins to understand that her own political philosophy is very close to that of Earl Scruggs, then clearly something significant is about to occur.

Nobody in Nashville perceived that significance more clearly, or was heartened by it any more completely, than the hard-living, Christian expatriate from Dyess, Arkansas—Johnny Cash.

# 4

# JOHNNY CASH:
# Putting the Traditions
# Back Together

**Just so we're reminded of the ones who are held back,
Up there in front, there oughta be a Man in Black.** ©
*—Johnny Cash*

It stands there on the left, a mile or two beyond the tacky frontiers of runaway suburbia, looking like an antebellum prop on a movie set. Unlike most recording studios in Nashville, which are jammed together in a spruced-up swatch of urban renewal turf, the House of Cash rises stately and alone against a backdrop of rolling Tennessee pastureland.

The grass is still bent from the dew, and the sound of a mockingbird echoes faintly across the hillsides as Johnny Cash's Cadillac glides into the parking lot. It is eight-thirty in the morning, a time of day that he would have dreaded a few years back—during the seven or eight years when he

54

would begin each day by gulping a handful of amphetamines.

He wasn't too particular about the dosage, two or three at a time, ten or fifteen milligrams a pop, dexedrine, benzedrine, dexamyl. It didn't much matter as long as they did their thing—as long as they helped him get from one concert to the next on the long road trips, and then, finally, as long as they helped him exist from one miserable morning until the one that followed.

The side effects were predictably squalid. He would pace the floor until the wee, desolate hours of semidawn, until finally barbiturates would bring him down and lull him into a nightmarish sleep. He developed a nervous twitch in his neck, and apparently in his brain as well, judging from some of the things he did as his metabolism ran its tortured course from uppers to downers and back again.

He was arrested and jailed seven times, on charges ranging from public drunkenness to buying drugs from illegal sources. On one of his stops in jail—in Carson City, Nevada—only an impromptu version of "Folsom Prison Blues" managed to pacify an unglued lumberjack whose avowed intention was to strangle his more famous cellmate.

He once crashed through a warning gate at a U. S. Navy bombing range and drove four miles across a live mine field in the Mojave Desert. He drove tractors over cliffs, wrecked half a dozen expensive cars, and tore up his marriage. Yet somehow he managed to survive until 1968, when, as Kris Kristofferson puts it, "he got him a good woman" and found himself reintroduced to Jesus.

That reintroduction became a bedrock for him, and in the process it gave his music a sense of mission that grows stronger and stronger as time goes by. Whether it's singing protest songs about the plight of Indians, or doing free shows in racially tense prisons, or donating time and testimonials to Billy Graham's crusades, Cash is essentially giving expression to a brand of back-home Christianity that is far more subtle than most people might expect.

"Yeah, I guess that's true—that is what I'm trying to do," he agrees, as he munches on an apple in his wood-paneled office, his features ruddy and relaxed, and his trim, two-hundred-pound frame draped into an easy chair.

Cash does not give many interviews these days, but when he does, he participates fully and shows no traces of superstar pretensions. In the early

Opposite: Cash, himself, has seen both the bottom and the top. His face tells the story. (Photo by Mike Clemmer, *The Charlotte Observer*.)

Left: Johnny Cash and Bob Dylan embodied the 1960's reunification of American folk and country music. (Photo courtesy *The Nashville Tennessean*.)

Below: Johnny Cash has given dozens of free concerts in America's prisons, prompted in large measure, he explains, by his sense of Christian duty. (Photo be George L. Walker III.)

stages, in fact, his voice will display just a hint of the butterfly tremors that are there around the edges when he walks on stage before five thousand people. But launching into an answer is like launching into a song, and his presence becomes certain and commanding as he begins to discuss, say, the relationship between his religion and his legendary concerts at several dozen prisons.

"The only prison concert I ever got paid for," he explains in a baritone voice that's as rich and ringing up close as it is on record, "was the one I did in Huntsville, Texas, in 1957. I took the show to the other ones free, I hope as my Christianity in action. I don't usually talk about that, and I wouldn't now if you hadn't asked me. I don't think a Christian oughta brag about his deeds, and anyway it's something that's meant a lot to me."

He peels off another chunk of apple with his black-handled pocketknife and then begins warming to the subject. "There are a lot of people who don't understand what's happened to me," he says. "They say Cash used to be tough and now he's soft. The truth is I'm a lot tougher now. What those people don't understand is that the old Johnny Cash would have literally died in sixty-six or sixty-seven if it hadn't been for faith.

"Faith is the foundation of everything I do. It's what I am. It always has been, really. There was just a time when I wasn't living it very well."

Cash, unlike some of his fellow fundamentalists, does not usually begin such monologues on his own. He is not a heavy-handed proselytizer, at least not with words, for he understands full well the tedium of holier-than-thou sermons. But his Christianity is a serious thing, as are the morals and values that have been tied up with it ever since his boyhood days in Dyess, Arkansas.

He was raised in a five-room, wood-frame house in the sultry cotton country of the delta. The Depression was in full force, but his father, Ray Cash, always seemed to make enough of a crop to feed his own family and to bail out needy neighbors as well. There was an ethos of sharing in those days that intertwined very logically with the deification of hard work.

Dyess, in fact, was founded on precisely that combination of principles. It was an FDR experiment—a socialistic farmers' cooperative with a store, cotton gin, and cannery that belonged to the farmers themselves. According to the plan, the co-op members would bring their edible crops to the cannery, and after the processing was completed they would get back eight of every ten cans. The other two would be sold to keep the project going, and if there were any profits at the end of the year, the co-op members would divide them.

Times were much too hard to permit any philosophical ramblings about the ideologies that were being practiced. But young John Cash was deeply influenced—permanently, as it turned out—by a curious meshing of the Protestant work ethic, a Golden Rulish empathy for people in need, and the visceral, unabashed fundamentalism of an Arkansas Church of God.

All of that has stamped his music with a distinctive tension, a creative tug-of-war between toughness and sentimentality, idealism and earthiness, that has enabled him to reach an impressive array of people and emotions. He could stroll onstage at San Quentin, for example, and sing a few old spirituals like "Peace in the Valley," tugging on the heartstrings and the latent, laid-away softness that does not usually show itself behind the walls of a prison—and then he could break suddenly into one of the most ruthless and hard-hitting prison songs that many of the inmates had ever heard:

> San Quentin, I hate every inch of you
> You cut me and you scarred me through and through
> San Quentin, may you rot and burn in hell
> May your walls fall and may I live to tell
> May all the world forget you ever stood
> And may all the world regret you did no good ©

Cash saw no contradiction between the feelings expressed in the spirituals and prison songs, or for that matter between the various kinds of stages where he was asked to play—from Richard Nixon's White House, to the Ryman Auditorium, to the annual folk festival in Newport, Rhode Island. It all fit together deep in his instincts, and to understand how, it helps to spend an unhurried hour or two in his tastefully posh, second-floor office at the House of Cash.

The trappings around the room will tell you a lot—a Holy Bible in the middle of a heavy oak coffee table, and next to it a paperback collection of Appalachian protest songs, *Voices From the Mountains*.

On a table off to the side is a stack of testimonial books from born-again

Christians (topping the stack, appropriately enough, is Chuck Colson's *Born Again*), and on the wall behind his desk are five color photographs that he took himself. Three are close-ups of his family—his second wife, June, and his young son, John Carter; and then a pair of nature shots that may or may not be intentionally symbolic—a hummingbird hovering near a dew-covered blossom, and a gnarled and wind-blown cottonwood tree, clinging to life in the deserts of New Mexico.

Still another photograph, less predictable than the rest, leans next to the desk in a stained wooden frame. It's an autographed enlargement of a Bob Dylan album cover, with an inscription that reads: "To John and June, Love, Bob Dylan."

It turns out that Dylan and Cash go back a long way, to the days when the fans of folk and the fans of country found themselves on opposite sides of a deepening political chasm—one group focusing on the nation's inequalities and shortcomings, the other on its promise and prosperity. The folkies were younger and luckier. They had that crucial combination of intelligence, sensitivity, and economic security that made it possible to question the status quo; and when they did, they found a lot of answers that were not very satisfying.

The fans of country, meanwhile, had come out the other side of a ferocious depression and a couple of wars with their patriotism stirred and their standard of living on a steady path upward. They not only believed, they *knew*, that the country couldn't be nearly as badly off as its critics were contending. They became increasingly defensive and bitter, and before the shouting match was over it brought out some of the ugliest instincts that both sides had to offer.

At least that was generally true. But there were, of course, exceptions, and Cash was among them. He saw no problem in focusing on problems as well as prosperity, believing that the commonality of the American experience went deeper than even the most serious of political divisions. He came at that understanding through his musical intuitions, and the process began in earnest back in 1962, when Columbia Records released an album entitled *The Free-Wheelin' Bob Dylan*.

It contained some of Dylan's best-known originals—"Blowin' in the Wind," "Don't Think Twice" (which Cash later recorded), and a bitter protest anthem called "Masters of War." All of them were done in Dylan's peculiar, talking-blues style that soon turned the folk world on its ear. Cash, however, heard the album a little bit differently from most of Dylan's other admirers.

"I didn't know him back then," he remembers, casting a glance towards Dylan's likeness, "but I liked the album so much I wrote him a letter—got his address from Columbia Records [which is also Cash's label] and I congratulated him on a fine country record. I could hear Jimmie Rodgers in his record, and Vernon Dalhart from back in the twenties, the whole talking-blues genre. I said, 'You're about the best country singer I've heard in years.'

"He wrote back and seemed kind of flabbergasted," Cash continues. "He said, 'I remember one time back in Hibbing, Minnesota, in 1957, you were there and I was one of the people out there listening.' He said, 'All during the 50s, it was you and Hank Williams.'"

The letters were the start of a steady correspondence that cemented a sense of soul brotherhood even before the two singers met at the Newport Folk Festival in 1963. Theirs quickly became one of the most remarkable friendships in American music, and in some ways one of the pivotal expressions of Dylan's humaneness and Cash's Christianity.

Both performers recognized that the political divisions between their fans were far from frivolous, tied as they were to such issues as war and peace and residues of prejudice. But in their music at least—and therefore in the deeper and instinctive aspirations of the people who listen—the two performers sensed a similar groping for the same universals.

In addition to Dylan's nonpolitical songs of rambling, Cash could identify strongly with a peaceful anthem like "Blowin' In The Wind." He had recorded his share of songs like it, and some that were even more obviously angry.

One of the angriest was "The Ballad of Ira Hayes," written by an Indian songwriter named Peter LaFarge, and telling a true story that had become bitterly symbolic to a rising generation of young Indian militants. Hayes had been a marine during World War II, and during the Battle of Iwo Jima hill he was one of a handful of men to make it to the top and help plant the American flag. The photo of Old Glory on the rise became one of the classics of World War II, and when Hayes returned home to his native Arizona, he received a short-lived hero's welcome.

But, as the song says, "He was just a Pima Indian," and he returned to the reservation, where jobs were scarce and where water that had once flowed into ancient Pima irrigation ditches had been diverted to serve the growing city of Phoenix. Without either work or hope, Hayes became a drunk, and one night as he staggered toward home he passed out and drowned in a muddy irrigation ditch with two inches of water in the bottom.

Cash recorded a whole album of songs about such Indian tragedies, but he also wrote and sang about other subjects that struck far closer to home for most of his audience. During the height of the protests against the war in Vietnam, he wrote a song that offered a blunt chastisement of those who were closing their ears and minds to the voices of the young. "What Is Truth?" went like this:

> **A little boy of three sittin' on the floor**
> **Looks up and says, "Daddy, what is war?"**
> **"Son, that's when people fight and die."**
> **A little boy of three says, "Daddy, why?"**
> **Young man of 17 in Sunday School**
> **Being taught the Golden Rule**
> **And by the time another year's gone around**
> **It may be his turn to lay his life down.**
> **Can you blame the voice of youth for asking**
> **What is truth? ©**

The odd thing was that the song was a hit on the country charts, and the reason, Cash thinks, is that even in his most protesty songs, he never traveled far down the road to ideology—never let his music depart from its basically Christian, humane roots to become the political property of any one faction. He was very literal-minded about the points of origin. If the subject was war, his takeoff point was the Sixth Commandment or the Sermon on the Mount. If he was performing in a prison, his inspiration was Luke 4:18 about Jesus and the captives. It was neat and simple, which suited Cash fine. He had already learned from his pill-popping days that his life didn't work when he lost sight of his moorings.

But the political factions didn't understand all of that, and they worked very hard to claim Cash as their own. Richard Nixon invited him to appear at the White House and, through H. R. (Bob) Haldeman, asked him to sing two of the most conservative songs of the era—Merle Haggard's "Okie from Muskogee," and a reactionary recitation called "Welfare Cadillac," written on a whim by an amateur songwriter named Guy Drake.

Cash politely refused to sing either song, much to the delight of his growing following of college kids. But much to their simultaneous disappointment, he pointedly refrained from criticizing either Nixon or the songs themselves—explaining instead that he didn't know "Welfare Cadillac," and that he was sure Nixon would soon invite Haggard himself to sing "Okie from Muskogee."

"I try not to become involved in politics," Cash explains today, and in a narrow sense that's certainly true. But in a larger sense it isn't, for Cash began to understand that people saw him as a reconciling force—a person whose music and presence could somehow reach beneath the anger and divisions.

He genuinely believed that there was something more basic about the country than its polarized factions, and the symbol of that conviction became his network television show on ABC. It began in the fall of 1969, and during the course of the two seasons it lasted Cash managed to plug such country artists as the Statler Brothers, Doug Kershaw, Charley Pride, and a struggling young songwriter named Kris Kristofferson.

But equally significant in his own mind was his attempt to introduce his country fans to the folk artists many of them might have expected to despise: Bob Dylan, Pete Seeger, Arlo Guthrie, and Judy Collins, to name a few.

"A lot of people got their first look at American folk on my country show," Cash remembers with a satisfied smile. "I thought at first we might get some flak for it, but we didn't really. Only Pete Seeger was an issue because of his politics. But I just told the network he was a fine performer and writer, and a legend in folk music. His stand on ecology I appreciated. I just said I wanted him on the show. It wasn't a big deal really. I saw that country and folk had a lot in common."

Cash wasn't the only one to reach that conclusion. On the other side of the fence, Bob Dylan began feeling enough of a kinship with the music of Nashville to begin making his records there. The idea jelled for a variety of reasons—not the least of which was the influence of his producer, Bob Johnston, who was also the producer for Johnny Cash and shared a belief in the musical compatibility of country and folk.

In addition, Dylan himself had already developed a healthy professional respect for Nashville's legendary sessions pickers—among them Charley McCoy, Wayne Moss, Pig Robbins, and Henry Strezlecki. McCoy had played on one of Dylan's New York sessions (handling acoustic guitar work on "Desolation Row") and Dylan was impressed with what he heard. So he came to Nashville in 1966, arriving one afternoon about six o'clock and asking the assembled musicians—Moss, McCoy, Strezlecki, Robbins, Kenny Buttrey, and Fred Carter, Jr.—to hang loose while he finished writing a song called "Sad-Eyed Lady of the Lowlands."

"About 4 A.M.," remembers McCoy, "he was ready to record."

The musicians didn't mind the wait; they were being paid for their time. But they were at first stunned and then deeply impressed by Dylan's unique combination of casualness and a single-minded determination to make the best possible music whatever the cost.

"Really," says Moss, "we used to think of Nashville sessions as being relaxed, but Dylan changed our whole approach. He was so relaxed and laid-back that your creative juices took on an entirely different aspect. He took the time to think the session out. Anything we wanted to try, it was have at it. He was very critical of himself, not so much of the musicians around him."

Dylan made three more recording trips to Nashville, and each time he found himself more and more drawn to the city's musical style. The culmination of that attraction was his *Nashville Skyline* album, which relied heavily on such distinctively country sounds as Pete Drake's steel guitar.

But if Dylan's affection for Nashville seemed to grow with each of his visits, the same was also true of Nashville's affection for Dylan. Almost everyone associated with the *Nashville Skyline* sessions—from the musicians to engineer Neil Wilburn—was impressed by Dylan's soft-spoken courtesy and thoughtfulness. And the result of that impression was a sort of ad hominem-in-reverse analysis of his politics. If he's such a decent person, people began to say, maybe we shouldn't be offended by the things he believes.

"That's one of the great things music can do," concludes Charley McCoy. "If you take a controversial subject, politicians can tell you what they think and you'll get mad. Somebody can put it in a song and you love it."

Johnny Cash believed that too, and McCoy, Dylan, and nearly anyone else around Nashville will tell you that there was nobody any better at proving the point. Cash would wander onstage at the rickety old Ryman, the late-night crowd a little bleary around the eyes but moving toward the point where fatigue gives way to a second wind of rebel yells.

Clad in his ruffled white shirt and Lincolnesque dress suit, he would run through a kind of autobiography in song: from lonely-times ballads like Kristofferson's "Sunday Morning Coming Down" to the gospel songs of his later years, delivered in a rich, flat voice that sounds as if it's welded to the lyrics.

During one of those appearances, on March 15, 1974—the last performance of the Grand Ole Opry before it moved to its slick new quarters at Opryland—Cash paused briefly in the middle of his set and ad-libbed an introduction to a pair of new songs. His voice showed traces of uncertainty, as if he were not sure how much to say. Then he cut the explanation short and let the music speak for itself.

The first song was also the oldest, a piece called "Man in Black," written in 1971 before a concert at Vanderbilt University. It was intended to be a statement of his political philosophy, he said, and as the spotlight narrowed and focused on his face, these were the words he began to sing:

> I wear the black of the poor and the beaten down,
> Livin' in the hopeless, hungry side of town,
> I wear the black for the prisoner who has long paid for his crime
> But is there because he's a victim of the times.
>
> I wear black for those who never read,
> Or listened to the words that Jesus said,
> About the road to happiness thru love and charity,
> Why, you'd think He's talking straight to you and me. ©

As the lyrics poured out, the old men with wrinkled faces and the scabs of fresh razor nicks sat ramrod straight and squinted toward the stage as if it were crescendo time in the preacher's sermon. The good ole boys decided to ease off for a while on the rebel yells, and the ladies with the piled-up hair and the Instamatic cameras let their flashbulbs fall temporarily silent.

Cash had gotten inside them the way he always does, providing some fodder for their serious thoughts, a tug or two at their laid-away feelings. But then, to underscore the point that he was still one of them, and to deepen their understanding of what was on his mind, he quickly shifted gears and moved into a song called "Ragged Old Flag."

It's a poignant pledge of allegiance, the story of an old man sitting in a small-town square, gazing at the tattered flag that flies above the courthouse and speculating about all the things that it and the country have been through together.

"I don't like to brag," the old man tells a stranger, "but we're mighty proud of that ragged old flag."

It was a triumphant night for Johnny Cash, one of many in the early seventies. But even as the applause was ringing in his head, he also knew, as he later wrote in his autobiography, that he was nearing the end of a chapter. With a little help from his friends, the pieces of his own life had been put back together, and there were some early indications that the country was moving in the same direction. So he began to enter a period of reflection, of savoring the moments with his family, and of exploring a feeling of contentment that he hadn't often known since the years of his boyhood.

And yet, strangely enough, it proved to be a time of peculiar nonsuccess. For the better part of two years, until the summer of 1976, every record he released turned out to be a flop. "I just got lazy," says Cash if you ask him why. But if that's what it was, he seems to have found a new burst of energy. A string of hits including "One Piece at a Time" and "That Old Time Feeling" signaled the beginning, he thinks, of some new stage.

Cash says he has no preconceptions about where the stage will lead him. But if he can mix some commercial success with his peace of mind, then the long, hard trip will have all been worth it. And in any event, he says with matter-of-fact conviction, it's all in the hands of the Lord.

# 5

# IN THE WAKE OF JOHNNY CASH:
## New Writers & New Ideas

I remember all those nights in good ole Nashville
Hangin' out with all them country stars
Ain't no better nights than nights in Nashville
Makin' music on my old guitar. ©

—*Hoyt Axton*

One Saturday night in 1970, George Hamilton IV got a call from Joni
Mitchell. She was in Nashville, she explained, to do a taping of the Johnny
Cash show, but in the meantime she was having some pickers out to her
motel room for a late-night jam session.

She invited Hamilton to come along, which was not the least bit
surprising. He had been one of the first performers in any musical field to
have a major hit with a Joni Mitchell song, and it had happened quite by
accident. One night on his way back to Nashville from North Carolina, he

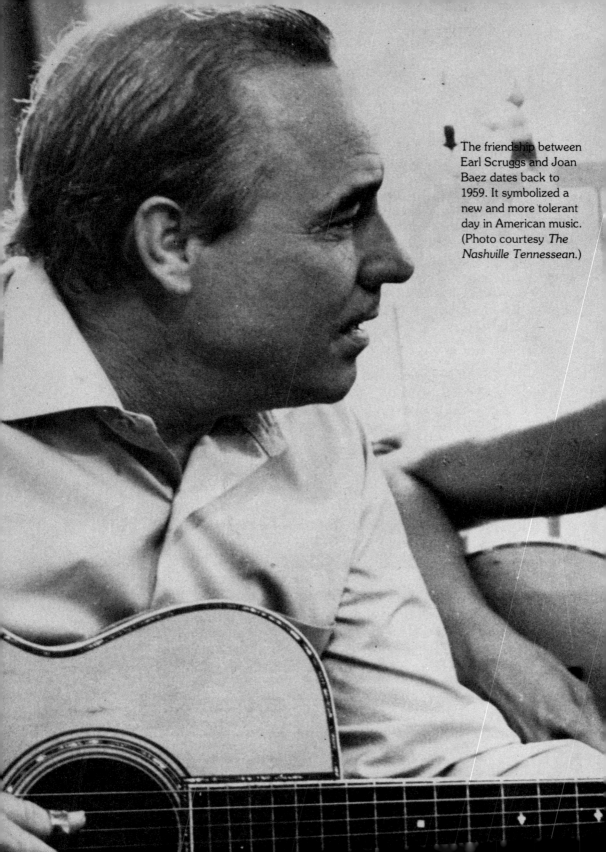

The friendship between Earl Scruggs and Joan Baez dates back to 1959. It symbolized a new and more tolerant day in American music. (Photo courtesy *The Nashville Tennessean*.)

Kris Kristofferson arrived in Nashville as a short-haired one-time Rhodes Scholar and Army brat. He emerged as one of the city's most skillful writers—producing what Bill Anderson calls a handful of "perfect songs." (Photo courtesy The Country Music Foundation Library.)

Opposite: Kristofferson's appearance had changed by the time he performed at Willie Nelson's Fourth of July picnic in 1976. His music, however, had remained remarkably constant. (Photo courtesy Mounument Records and CBS Records.)

had been cruising along Interstate 40 listening to the car radio when Tom Rush came on with a song called "Urge For Going"—a Joni Mitchell original about good-byes and wanderlust that was laced with the kind of lyrical imagery that would soon make her famous.

Hamilton was impressed, tracked her down at a Charleston, South Carolina, coffeehouse, and got her to send him a tape. His version of the song made the Top Ten on the country charts, and for Joni it was a commercial breakthrough.

By the night of her Nashville jam session, however, she had become a star in her own right, and Hamilton was flattered to be included in the gathering—especially when he saw the people who were there. Along with Joni, there were rock singers Michael Nesmith, the talented member of a teenybopper heart-stopper group called the Monkess, and Graham Nash and David Crosby of Crosby, Stills, Nash and Young. From Nashville, in addition to Hamilton, were an up-and-coming songwriter named Mickey Newbury and a shy and somber unknown named Kris Kristofferson, who everybody said was going to be great.

"It was quite a night," Hamilton remembers, looking back from the perspective of six years later. "It was one of those famous exchange-of-songs sessions that were so common in Nashville in those days. Every time people like Joni would come through, they would get together with some local pickers, often out at Cash's house, but someplace, and they would listen to each other's songs.

"This particular session went on until the wee hours of Sunday morning, and then Joni turned to Kris, who had been just sitting there quietly while everybody else played, and she said, 'You haven't played anything yet, Kris.' He mumbled some 'aw shucks' reply about how he wasn't a singer, but everybody insisted, so he pulled out a notebook and said he had a couple of new ones and he'd have to read 'em.

"He sang 'Me and Bobby McGee' and 'Sunday Morning Coming Down.' I'll never forget it. There he was, a bashful newcomer with his short hair, no beard, and button-down collar; and I mean it wasn't an act. That's how he really was, a really genuine kind of person reading his songs out of a notebook while he strummed on his guitar.

"When he finished with those two, there were maybe 60 seconds of total silence. Everybody knew it was the best two songs that were done that night. People were thinking, 'Who the hell is this?' And yet everybody knew he was the best in the room. Nash and Crosby told him to look them up if he ever got out to the Coast, and he mumbled something about how Cash or maybe Roger Miller had said something about cutting some of his stuff. Pretty soon both of them did, and after that, he was on his way.

"It was a beautiful period in Nashville."

And so it was. Kristofferson hit town about the same time as a few dozen other like-minded young writers—people like Newbury, Willis Hoover, Vince Matthews, and John Hartford—all of whom had grown up in the Bob Dylan-Gordon Lightfoot era of songwriting but had clung to a stubborn, undiminished appreciation of Hank Williams and Lefty Frizzell.

There was a sort of respectful rebelliousness about Kris and his cronies, and even in the early years, when they were scratching for their meals in the run-down rooming houses, there was a sense of excitement about their coming. They weren't making any money; their songs were being cut only sporadically, if at all. But they were immersing themselves in the life of Nashville, and drawing in return a good bit of emotional sustenance.

Mythology has it that the powers of the industry were initially indifferent, and at the boardroom, coat-and-tie level, that was largely the case. But at the artist level, it was not, and as Kristofferson looks back today, the things that stand out for him are the late-night jam sessions with the established writers and performers—Johnny Cash, Willie Nelson, and Harlan Howard, among others.

Howard, especially, was a fan of his protégés. He had established himself long before as one of the most skillful writers of straight country songs—"Busted," "Pick Me Up On Your Way Down," and hundreds more that weave authentic emotions through simple structures—but he would hang out at the Professionals Club with Kristofferson and the hungries, and he would tell them with absolute conviction: "If Nashville is going to progress, it's going to be because of you and you and you; not Willie and me."

Johnny Cash had a similar reaction, and Kristofferson and the other young writers will tell you—in tones that often lapse into reverence—that there was nobody any more generous or energetic in pushing their cause. Cash, however, is inclined to remember his own role in more modest terms.

"Kristofferson was carrying out wastebaskets at Columbia studios, about 1966 sometime," he says. "I had a lot of sessions that year, and he always managed to get his work scheduled when I was recording. He could be carrying out trash at two in the morning.

"He had been told not to plug his songs to me while I was recording. I didn't even know all that; he told me about it later. Finally, he got to slipping the tapes to June (she and I weren't married yet), and I'd sit up all night long listening. I thought, 'Anything this good can't be commercial.'

"'Sunday Morning Coming Down' was the story of my life at that time. He had another one called 'The Best of All Possible Worlds,' which is about getting thrown into jail, and I heard it right after I got out. I held on to his songs for three or four years before I ever recorded any of them. That didn't do him any good, but they were just too personal for me at the time.

"Then I went on network TV and I was no longer in and out of jails, and I could look at Kristofferson songs with the mind of a performer or an artist; they became something I could sing without it hurtin' so bad."

So Cash took Kristofferson with him to the Newport Folk Festival, put him on his network show, and recorded "Sunday Morning Coming Down." Roger Miller did "Me and Bobby McGee," and soon afterward Kris began cutting his own albums for Monument Records and winning songwriting awards from the Country Music Association. He was on his way, and before long he had become the key figure in a crucial new trend for country music, a kind of broadening of both audiences and influences that has had a lot to do with where the music is heading today.

He wasn't the only one, of course, and in fact he wasn't even the first to hit it big. If you had to pick a breakthrough song, a lot of people in Nashville maintain that it was "Gentle On My Mind," written by a lackadaisical Nashville disc jockey named John Hartford, who would probably have done a little better in radio if his mind hadn't been constantly a-jumble with the snatches and fragments of songs that he was trying to whip into shape.

"Gentle On My Mind" was one that worked—a quintessential blend of influences that sounds in part like a Jimmie Rodgers hobo song, and yet has the kind of poetic imagery associated with Gordon Lightfoot or Joni Mitchell.

> **It's just knowing that the world will not be cursing or forgiving**
> **When I walk along some railroad track and find**
> **That you're moving on the backroads, by the rivers of my mem'ry**
> **And for hours, you're just gentle on my mind.***

The same combination of qualities was present in abundance in Kristofferson's "Me and Bobby McGee," Willis Hoover's "Freedom To Stay," Billy Joe Shaver's "Ride Me Down Easy." And so the young writers began breaking down walls, drawing a more youthful and intellectual audience into the fringes of the country tradition. It was true, of course, that many of the newer fans were reluctant to admit what was happening. They might like Mickey Newbury or Kris Kristofferson, but they thought of them as folk or rock—anything but country—and the squeamishness wouldn't end for several more years.

But the new-country writers were an affront to stereotyped expectations of all descriptions, and nobody relished that position any more than Mickey Newbury. He was dismayed by the fact that the fans of country music were reluctant to identify with the peaceful sentiments of a song like "Blowin' In the Wind"—that many of them, being deeply mistrustful of the politics of Bob Dylan, refused to accept his music for the things that it said. But he also knew there were no monopolies on closed-mindedness, and he had, if anything, even less patience with the semi-hip coffeehouse crowds who regarded country music as some kind of boorish anachronism that was a little too hard on sophisticated ear drums.

One night in the late sixties, he was appearing at the Bitter End West in Los Angeles, and he began discussing such matters backstage with comedian David Steinberg. It was a time of frequent newspaper headlines about whites in newly integrated Southern schools insisting on "Dixie" as the school fight song, and blacks protesting because to them it was an anthem of white supremacy.

Newbury was annoyed because he saw nothing in the song itself that should make it the exclusive property of one-time segregationists, and on a whim he announced that he would sing it that night just to prove a point.

* Copyright © 1967 and 1968 by Ensign Music Corporation. Used by permission of the copyright owner.

The Bitter End's manager, Paul Colby, was alarmed at the prospect—at first laughing nervously on the off-chance that Newbury was joking. But when he realized that the star of the evening was absolutely serious, he began explaining with rapid-fire urgency that "Dixie" was not exactly the type of song that a bunch of radicalized young Californians had turned out to hear.

No matter. Newbury was undeterred, and when he got onstage he ran through part of his normal set, and then with a gentle strum of his guitar, he began to sing the words, "Oh I wish I was in the land of cotton." But instead of belting them out in the rebel-yell style that everybody was accustomed to, he plucked the notes slowly on his old guitar, and his voice took on a rich, haunting quality that called up a different set of images—visions not of a mean-spirited South, but of a poignant South, a land caught in the grips of tragedy and suffering for 150 years.

There was power in the transformation, and it grew even stronger as Newbury shifted in midnote to "The Battle Hymn of the Republic," and then to an antebellum gospel song called "All My Trials." Before the impromptu trilogy was completed, it had become one of the most supercharged events in the history of the Bitter End West. Every other sound in the room had vanished in the emotion of the moment. Odetta, the famous black folksinger, was sitting in the front row with tears in her eyes, and Newbury knew that he had accomplished his purpose and a great deal more.

Johnny Cash and others believe there was a special power about the new-country performers, unleashed by a fusing of traditions—the reunification of country and folk, and the sharing of wisdom that each had picked up during the years of estrangement.

Country music, says Cash, is by far the better for it, and a wide range of people agree with him. Bill Anderson, for example, a writer of deliberately unsubtle songs, believes that in the years following the appearance of Newbury and Kristofferson (whom he regards as two of the most influential songwriters ever) "country music has done the things that it's always done even better."

"Kristofferson," adds Anderson in a search for the strongest superlative he can muster, "is the modern-day Hank Williams. He has written about a half dozen perfect songs. And that, believe me, is a lot."

But if country music was influenced for the better by other traditions, the reverse was also true. Joan Baez, for example, began recording in Nashville in the late sixties, and as much as any other folky (except perhaps Lightfoot or Tyson) she began doing what Charley McCoy calls "a real Nashville kind of session." She used home-grown pickers like Norman Blake and Jerry Reed, and she began recording Nashville material—songs by Kristofferson, Steve Young, Willie Nelson, and Mickey Newbury, to name a few.

She also recorded her first hit single, a song called "The Night They Drove Old Dixie Down," which at first must have seemed wildly out of character to many of her fans. It's a song about the fall of the South in 1865, and it laments the suffering connected with the Southern defeat—the emotional wrenchings, deaths, and physical privations associated with the losing of a cause.

It doesn't deal with the question of whether the cause was just, and in that sense it's far less political than many of the songs for which Baez is noted. And yet, in many ways it is one of the more eloquent antiwar numbers that she ever recorded—touching a level of feeling that is universally human and beyond political abstraction.

Nashville had that effect on a lot of protest singers. It offered a reintroduction to the decent simplicity of the country tradition, and to understand the importance of that reintroduction you need only listen to the sentimental but heart-felt lyrics of Joan Baez's "Outside Nashville City Limits."

She had written the song after a December drive in the country with Kris Kristofferson, in which she had wound up at the farm of Marijohn Wilkin. Marijohn had written a standard called "Long Black Veil" that Baez had recorded on an early album. It sounded like an old British folk ballad, but Marijohn and her husband are alive-and-kicking Tennessee country folk—peaceful people, whose salt-of-the-earth values seemed strangely compatible with the radical visions of Joan Baez.

This, in part, is what Joan wrote after the visit was over:

> **Outside the Nashville city limits a friend and I did drive**
> **On a day in early winter I was glad to be alive.**
> **We went to see some friends of his who lived upon a farm**

Strange and gentle country folk who wished nobody harm
Fresh-cut 60 acres, eight cows in the barn.
But the thing that I remember on that cold day in December
Was that my eyes they did brim over as we talked.

In the slowest drawl I'd ever heard the man said come with me
Y'all want to see the prettiest place in all of Tennessee
He poured us each a glass of wine and a'walking we did go
Along fallen leaves and cracklin' ice where a tiny brook did flow
He knew every inch of the land and lord he loved it so
But the thing that I remember on that cold day in December
Was that my eyes were brimming over as we walked. ©

Still another deep impression on Baez came from Earl Scruggs. They had met as mutual admirers at the 1959 Newport Folk Festival (shyly doing a duet of "Wildwood Flower"), but it was only after Joan began her recording visits to Nashville that they began to find time for serious conversation. During one such talk, they began to discuss the war in Vietnam, and Joan approached the topic a little bit gingerly— understanding full well that a great many people in country music were vehemently opposed to her left-of-center views.

On the issue of the war, though, she was surprised to discover that she and Scruggs were in substantial agreement. He told her that he didn't want his teenaged sons to kill or be killed in Southeast Asia, and that he would support whatever they decided to do about the war because they were his boys.

Scruggs underscored the point dramatically in 1969 when he joined Baez, Arlo Guthrie, and a few other champions of protest at the Moratorium March on Washington—demanding an end to the killing. Though he concedes that there may have been a few raised eyebrows among some of his Grand Ole Opry colleagues back in Nashville, Scruggs says today that he has no regrets.

"That's not really my thing, protest marches," he explains in the rich Southern accents he acquired as a boy in North Carolina. "But I had occasion back in the late sixties to talk to somebody close to President Nixon's administration, and he told me it was worth thirty-thousand more lives to prolong the war until the 1972 elections.

"Well, I'm a patriot, and being critical of my country doesn't come easy to me. But that just about made me sick. I believe a person should speak his convictions peacefully, and that's what I did. I don't know what people said behind my back, but as far as to my face, I never felt any repercussions at all."

"I don't think there were any," says Scruggs's Opry colleague Minnie Pearl. "People respected it. We knew Earl."


What the Earl Scruggs episode indicated was that the politics of country music were a great deal more diverse than people like Joan Baez might have expected. They knew that the music—like everything else in America in the late sixties and early seventies—had become increasingly politicized, but the most common images were of country stars like Billy Grammer and Sam McGee campaigning ardently for George Wallace.

There were exceptions. Scruggs was one, George Hamilton IV was another (he did a concert for Robert Kennedy in 1968), and there was even a Nashville songwriter named Shirl Milete who wrote and recorded a sympathetic lament about draft dodgers fleeing to Canada. There was a good reason for Milete's sympathies, for he happens to be a burly, tattooed good ole boy who believes very deeply that all war is wrong. On the basis of that belief, he refused to serve in Korea during the conflict there and subsequently did a stint in prison.

But obviously Milete was an exception—a fact underscored by the hard and cold reality that as far as he knows, not one single radio station ever played his record. Far more prominent were records such as Bobby Bare's "God Bless America Again," Bill Anderson's "Where Have All the Heroes Gone," and Merle Haggard's "Okie from Muskogee."

The latter song especially is a classic, uncompromising reaction to the feelings of antipatriotism that seemed to be rampant at the time. Haggard, like most of his fans, was deeply offended by such feelings—by the notion that a bunch of self-righteous kids who had never had to scratch, claw, or battle to make ends meet would smoke pot, burn draft cards, and generally reject—in the shrillest way possible—most of the values that seemed to glue the country together. To understand the depth of the reaction, you needed only to be in the crowd at a Merle Haggard concert and listen to the whoops of approval as his baritone voice began to belt out the lyrics:

**We don't smoke marijuana in Muskogee**
**We don't take our trips on LSD**
**We don't burn our draft cards down on Main Street**
**We like livin' right and bein' free.***

About the same time, Bill Anderson came out with "Where Have All the Heroes Gone," which bemoaned the absence of suitable example-setters for American youth, and contained some tough-talking put-downs of longhairs, black militants, and assorted other radicals and dissidents. Like "Okie From Muskogee," it was a smash, and Anderson, who grew up very Southern and conservative in the towns of Columbia, South Carolina, and Decatur, Georgia, was proud of it.

Gradually, however, both Anderson and Haggard began to mellow in their feelings, and by the midseventies, as the Bicentennial season rolled around, Anderson would wince a little when he heard his song on the radio, and he had stopped doing it in his concerts. In its place was a different kind of anthem, called "My Country," which in its own way is at least as patriotic as "Where Have All The Heroes Gone?"

The newer song, written by New England songwriter Jud Strunk, begins about the way you would expect—with vignettes and word pictures about America's beauty. But soon you realize that Strunk has woven a more complex tapestry, slipping in references to war, poverty, ghetto desperation, and political assassination—subjects that, until fairly recently, many country fans preferred not to dwell on.

Martin Luther King is extolled explicitly, and the conditions that impelled him to act are acknowledged freely. But the anthem ends on a note that leaves the crewcuts nodding in slow affirmation: "I may not stand for everything my country's about," it says, "but I do stand for my country."

"I really love that song," explains Anderson, "because it's not so red, white, and blue that it turns people off. It's not that I wanted to get away

* Copyright © 1969 Blue Book Music. Used by permission. All rights reserved.

completely from the feelings in 'Heroes.' I still think America needs heroes. But I've changed. My thinking has changed too. Some of the things early in 'Heroes' generalized about long hair, for example. It put down some people a little too hard. I haven't done it now in several years.

"I guess," Anderson continued in the soft and sincere voice that's become his trademark, "I feel sort of like Johnny Cash, who says he's 'born a little every day' and that once he stops learning and changing he starts dying. I think you see the same kind of change in the country-music audience. The audience is broadening, for one thing; it's pulling in more young people, thanks to performers like Kris Kristofferson.

"And the fan who has always been a fan, his horizons are broadening too. The truck driver today goes from Atlanta to maybe California, or Philadelphia, or Omaha. He doesn't just haul a load of chickens to Macon. He's seeing more and more of the country. It's bound to have an effect."

In short, Anderson concludes, partly because of the influence of young writers, and partly because of the times, country music has become intertwined with a bewildering set of changes on a number of fronts—politics, race, sex, religion, and the cultural gaps between traditional and newfound listeners. The way the music deals with all of those things is worth examining in some detail, beginning with one of the most profound and wrenching issues the country audience has ever had to face: the altered relationships between Americans who are white and those who are black.

The music, as usual, has proved deeply prophetic.

# 6

# BLACKS, BLUES & COUNTRY

**The blues was one thing we both understood.** ©

*—Merle Haggard*

Several years ago, a talented young Louisiana musician named Tony Joe White composed a song entitled "A Rainy Night in Georgia." The first big hit recording of it was done by a veteran black singer named Brook Benton, and as he wailed out the plaintive lyrics about being lonesome on a rainy night, you could see in your mind an aging, nomadic black man leaning against the side of a boxcar in his tattered clothes and with a head full of memories. In 1974, the song was redone—by Hank Williams, Jr.— and the image is just as clear: of a white hobo traveling to who knows where on a midnight train.

Maybe you don't think of blacks and country music together, but in the

Forty years before Charley Pride, DeFord Bailey was the first black star in country music. (Photo by George L. Walker III.)

Blind Nashville street-singer Cortelia Clark won a Grammy Award in 1967 for a brilliant, but obscure album called "Blues in the Streets." His name temporarily glittered in lights. (Photo courtesy *The Nashville Tennessean*.)

But Clark's sudden death and rain-spattered funeral soon inspired a country ballad by Mickey Newbury. (Photo courtesy *The Nashville Tennessean*.)

"The blues was one thing we both understood," sings Merle Haggard. This old man and his lonesome cup of coffee illustrate the truth of Haggard's song. (Photo by Steve Perille.)

There were hard times on both sides of the racial chasm in the South—a fact that deeply influenced country music as well as the blues. (Photo by Dot Jackson.)

Charlie Daniels (left), Willie Nelson (center) and blues fiddler Papa John Creach perform together in Nashville. (Photo by Bill Strode, *The Louisville Courier-Journal*.)

rural South the laments of blacks and whites have covered a lot of common ground. It probably should have come as less of a surprise than it did back in 1962 when Ray Charles, the acknowledged king of rhythm and blues, asked his producer, Sid Feller, to search out some quality country material for him to record. Feller, who had produced such Ray Charles classics as "What'd I Say" and "Georgia On My Mind," was a little stunned and apprehensive, despite the fact that Charles had begun his professional career, at age seventeen, as the fill-in piano player for a hack country band known as the Floriday Playboys.

All of that had been a long time ago, and in the intervening years Ray Charles had directed his considerable vocal talents toward expanding the audience for blues music from a relatively small collection of connoisseurs, who appreciated art for art's sake, and ghetto blacks, who were simply the refugees from the tar paper shacks and cotton fields where the music had begun. The earlier blues musicians—people like Leadbelly, Blind Boy Fuller, the Reverend Gary Davis, Howlin' Wolf, and Mississippi John Hurt—had all lived on the brink of poverty, some of them even on welfare, and with Ray Charles selling millions of records simply by sprucing up the rough edges, Sid Feller was profoundly skeptical of anything that smacked of new directions.

Nevertheless, he did as he was asked and came back with a collection of songs that included some of the biggest hits Ray Charles would ever record. And the ironic thing was that when "I Can't Stop Loving You," "Your Cheatin' Heart," and "Busted" (written respectively by Don Gibson, Hank Williams, and Harlan Howard) began climbing their way to the top of the charts, nobody talked about Ray Charles's changing tastes—and for a very good reason: He sounded almost exactly the same. His voice and his anguished interpretations were certainly no different, and the notes, chord progressions, and hard-time lyrics were remarkably compatible with those of his earlier records.

To Ray Charles, it was all very logical. "I've always loved Hillbilly music," he explained recently. "I never missed the Grand Ole Opry when I was young. Hillbilly music is totally honest. They don't sing, 'I sat there and dreamed of you.' They say, 'I missed you, and I went out and got drunk.' There are a lot of parallels between blues and country."

"Parallels" is the precisely accurate word, for the two musical forms historically have been as similar and yet as separate as the two cultures out of which they grew. Country was the music of redneck soul, and though the hopes and failures that gave it its power were inescapably intertwined with those that nourished the blues, the entire history of the South—at least until very recently—has been an attempt to deny that fact. Country was white, and the blues were black, and never the twain shall meet.

It is not surprising that it would be that way, for there have been few groups in American society who have been as openly hostile and fearful toward blacks as the traditional country-music audiences: Southern rednecks and working-class whites in the big cities of the North. But even in the years of peak segregation, the separation was never as complete as the mythology insisted it was. It was simply that cultural exchanges and other interracial dealings were carried out with such discretion and anonymity that whites were almost certain to come out on top. In the field of music, for example, such country notables as Merle Travis, Jimmie Rodgers, Chet Atkins, and Hank Williams all learned their music from obscure black men, whose obscurity was not the least bit lessened when their pupils went on to prominence.

The situation today, however, has begun to change. Musical segregation, like segregation in other spheres, is breaking down rapidly, and scenes like Dobie Gray or the Pointer Sisters playing to standing ovations at the Grand Ole Opry or going on tour with Tom T. Hall are becoming more and more commonplace. The Pointer Sisters' "Fairy Tale" hit the top of the country charts in 1974, a year after black singer Charley Pride had earned more money than any performer in the history of country music. In addition, the list of black singers who have recorded country material in their own styles is long and impressive, including among others in recent years Gladys Knight, Joe Simon, Brook Benton, Bobby Blue Bland and, of course, Ray Charles.*

* The exchanges have gone both ways in the 1970s. White country singer Freddy Weller had a major hit with Chuck Berry's "Promised Land," and Mickey Gilley did well with the old Sam Cooke song, "Bring It On Home to Me." A number of country artists have done the songs of the late Ivory Joe Hunter, a black writer in Memphis. During Hunter's long bout with cancer there was a benefit concert for him on the stage of the Opry, featuring Loretta Lynn and Isaac Hays.

This blending of black and white musical traditions implicitly alludes to what the lyrics of growing numbers of country songs are beginning explicitly to affirm: that Southerners are Southerners, and people are people, and skin color is not the most relevant distinction.

Perhaps the most poignant expression of this emerging point of view, and one that seems to appeal most effectively to the innate, down-home decency that dwells in much of the country-music audience, is Tom T. Hall's musical recitation, "I Want To See the Parade." The narrator of the story is a redneck who, out of sheer curiosity, had ambled on down to the site of a civil rights demonstration. As he was standing on the street corner, reflecting on the outrageousness of it all, he overheard a little girl behind him saying that she wished she could see the parade. He lifted her up in order to improve her vantage point, and when he did so, she hit him with a question that took him by surprise. "Mister," she said, "why does my daddy hate all those people going by?" As the redneck began to answer the question, he noticed that the little girl was blind, and when he looked around for an answer, "it was pretty hard to find."

"And that night," said the redneck, "I took a good look at myself, and this is the prayer I prayed: I said, 'Lord, I want you to hold *me* up. Cause *I* want to see the parade.'"

It is a simple but powerful piece of poetry, though in the real world, of course, the kind of enlightenment Hall describes is usually more evolutionary than instantaneous. It is often the product of a whole barrage of psychological influences, some of them subtle, some of them not so subtle, blending together over a period of time. One of those influences that worked its quiet and unobtrusive effect on the mind set of country music fans was the appearance in the midsixties of a new and very special superstar. Charley Pride, a free-spirited fugitive from the cotton-picking delta town of Sledge, Mississippi, burst upon the country scene at a time when many of his fans-to-be were frightened, uptight, and bitter about the civil rights revolution going on around them.

Pride, however, was uniquely equipped to soothe those fears. For one thing, his mellow, sunburned voice could just as easily have belonged to any of the fairer-skinned good ole boys who grew up down the road. And in addition to that, he had a certain aura, a sort of inoffensively perverse determination to do his own thing regardless of what others might say or think.

"I guess it's kind of funny, me being up here with this permanent tan," he would tell the Caucasian hordes who turned out to hear him never dreaming, from the sound of his recorded voice, that he was anything but one of them. And they would always relax, enjoy the show, and go out and buy more Charley Pride records.

Pride never meant to be a crusader, never intended to offer a self-conscious challenge to a bastion of whiteness (any more than he intended, a few years later, to strike a blow for social justice when he moved into an all-white, upper-class neighborhood in the suburbs of Dallas). But neither was he an Uncle Tom. He kept his dignity, and it probably did his audiences good to be confronted by a talented, self-contained son of Mississippi whose skin happened to be a different color from theirs.

Whatever the effect on his fans, the whole situation hasn't done Pride any harm. Country music has made him a lot richer and more famous than most of the home folks back in Sledge, and he's still modest enough to retain some feelings of gratitude—especially when he compares his situation, as he sometimes does, to that of DeFord Bailey.

Bailey, a black harmonica player, and one of the best who ever lived, was born at a bad time and became a star in country music about forty years too soon. He joined the cast of the Grand Ole Opry soon after its founding back in 1925, and was one of its most popular performers for sixteen years. In 1941, however, he was dropped from the cast on the dubious grounds that he hadn't written enough new songs (a fact that hadn't disturbed the Opry's executives until after they bought stock in a new song-licensing company called BMI).

For the next three decades after he left the Opry Bailey didn't perform very much, and made his living instead by shining shoes on a Nashville street corner. But the city fathers urban-renewed his shoe stand a few years back, and Bailey, now in his late seventies, spends his days in an antiseptic, old folks' high-rise near the vacant lot where the stand used to be. He says he still plays his harmonica a lot—"just about the same way some people smoke cigarettes."

It is not easy today to persuade DeFord Bailey to talk about the music industry that shafted him. He will sit there, dressed in his stiffly pressed blue suit, his felt hat, and his spotted tie, and he will parry every question expertly—always polite and smiling, but always noncommittal, unless he has seen some concrete reason to trust you. Few writers other than a young Vanderbilt University history student named David Morton have been able to establish such trust with Bailey, and when I took my own stab at it a little while back, I didn't come anywhere close.

But with Morton's help, I did manage to pull out one answer that may shed some light on the way he thinks. Asked if he would consider performing again, on the Opry stage or elsewhere, Bailey replied with a smile: "If they're talking right."

The topic of conversation he has in mind is money, and although there have been a number of negotiations on the subject in recent years, few have gotten anywhere. Bailey passed up a chance to cut an album with Pete Seeger even though he was offered a flat fee and a royalty percentage considerably in excess of the going rate. He turned down an offer to appear at the prestigious Newport Folk Festival, and most recently, according to David Morton, Bailey was offered $2,500 to play three songs in the Burt Reynolds movie *W. W. and the Dixie Dancekings*. He turned it down on the grounds that it wasn't enough.

"I don't want to give the impression that Mr. Bailey has been terribly difficult to deal with," says David Morton, who has become Bailey's friend, apologist, and unpaid manager. In fact, however, that impression is pretty close to accurate, and the reason would seem to be this: DeFord Bailey spent sixteen years as one of the biggest stars of the Grand Ole Opry, and throughout his tenure the Opry executives regarded him simply and explicitly as the institution's "mascot." He knows he is among the greatest harmonica players ever ("I was a humdinger," he says with a smile), and that knowledge is curiously liberating. He has nothing to prove and no apparent hunger for fame or money. If you want to hear him, then—simply as a matter of principle—you can pay his price. If you do not want to pay his price, there are no hard feelings but you will not hear him, and that is that.

It all sounds terribly arrogant, and it is. But most arrogance is tinged with a kind of feisty, uncertain quality, and DeFord Bailey's is not. He is one of the most gentlemanly, self-bemused, and delightedly self-assured people in the state of Tennessee. He is also nobody's fool. He has learned from his own experiences, and perhaps he has learned as well from the experiences of another black Nashville singer named Cortelia Clark, whose story is one of the most ironically tragic in the history of Nashville music.

Clark was a blind Negro streetsinger who spent a good part of his life on a downtown Nashville sidewalk, rasping out the blues while he played guitar and sold pencils for whatever amount people chose to drop into his tin cup. In 1967, however, when Clark was an old man, a young music producer named Mike Weesner came up with the idea of having him do an album. Arrangements were made with Chet Atkins of RCA, and the album, entitled *Blues in the Street*, was cut. It was a masterpiece. Critical acclaim was so high that Clark won a 1967 Grammy Award, and for at least a brief moment his name glittered in lights.

The only problem was that the album didn't sell. Clark made little money from it and soon found himself back on his downtown sidewalk selling pencils, his music nearly drowned out by the onrushing traffic.

I was a reporter for the Associated Press when Cortelia Clark was killed in a fire at his home a couple of years after his award. He was buried obscurely, at a rain-spattered funeral attended by only a few of his close friends. The poignancy of it all was a little overwhelming, so I worked at some length over a story about his life and teletyped it to the New York AP office for distribution over the national wires.

A few minutes later, the phone rang. It was the editor from New York. "Jesus Christ," he snapped in his nasal, Manhattan twang. "What do you think we're running—an obituary service for beggars?"

One person in Nashville who was particularly struck by the irony of Cortelia Clark's life was Mickey Newbury, a singer and songwriter now in his midthirties, who after years of quality work has begun to inch his way into the big time with such compositions as "An American Trilogy" and "San Francisco Mabel Joy." Newbury was raised on country music in the dusty back streets of Houston, Texas, but he is young enough to have been influenced in his musical tastes by other sources as well, among them

Bob Dylan and the protest singers of the sixties, and such relatively obscure blues musicians as Percy Mayfield and Cortelia Clark.

"I used to stop and listen to Cortelia," Newbury remembers. "I didn't know him well, never even knew his last name, but I admired him. I was out of town on the road when he died, and I just happened to be going through some old papers when I got back and stumbled on the story." Newbury says he mulled over the tragedy for quite some time, and his mulling finally produced a song that is one of the best of an emerging genre in country music: songs about the shared wisdom of blacks and whites in the rural South.

There are other examples: Tom T. Hall's recording about an aging black janitor who had come to see, in the course of his life, that the only things in the world worth very much at all are old dogs, children, and watermelon wine; Alex Harvey's composition about a "share-cropping colored man" who had befriended and cared for a little orphan white boy when no one else would do it; Donna Fargo's "Honey Chile," which speculates about what was once the most morbidly unthinkable possibility in the Southern subconscious: that if Jesus were black, there would be a whole bunch of Christians more deeply concerned about their immortality.

One other song in the same category is worth special mention because of the artist who sang it. A few years ago Johnny Russell, a fat and funny guitarist with a pleasant, powerful voice, turned out a song entitled "Catfish John," which told of a much-maligned friendship between a young white boy and a former black slave who had once been swapped by his owner for a Chestnut mare. It was Russell's biggest hit until 1974, when he released a record with the absolutely on-target, good-ole-boy country title of "Rednecks, White Socks, and Blue Ribbon Beer."

The song, which is set in a redneck bar, celebrates the way of life that its title connotes, and on the surface it is the sort of record that causes people like George Wallace and Richard Nixon to claim country music as their own special turf. Rednecks are simply assumed to be patriotic all-American vote fodder for conservative politicians, and any affiliation of redneckism—which Russell's song is—therefore is assumed to be a plus for the forces of reaction.

The most eloquent advancement of that theory came in a *Harper's Magazine* article in 1974, when a writer named Florence King condemned "Rednecks, White Socks and Blue Ribbon Beer" as a "truculent hymn to the twice-turned jockstrap that could someday become America's 'Horst Wessell.' The sullen defensiveness," she wrote, "becomes social dynamite when combined with the aggression inherent in songs of the Down-Home Patriotism category."

Richard Nixon phrased it a little differently in a Grand Ole Opry appearance a few months before his resignation, but his view was essentially the same. "In a serious vein for a moment," he said, "I want to say a word about what country music has meant to America. First, it comes from the heart of America. It talks about family. It talks about religion. And it radiates a love of this nation—a patriotism. Country music makes America a better country."

All of that is true as far as it goes, but people like Florence King and Richard Nixon are inclined to overlook at least one crucial point: that the patriotism of country music is no longer the utterly uncritical variety that both of them seem to believe it is. Country fans have experienced enough of the American dream to give them hope, but they have also felt the sting of its failings, have lived through Watergate and a recession, and the result is a peculiar set of populistic confusions. Merle Haggard may have written such intolerant anthems as "Okie From Muskogee" and "The Fightin' Side of Me," but he also wrote "If We Make It Through December," a fatalistic ballad about Christmastime factory layoffs, and "Hungry Eyes," a militant description of life in a migrant labor camp, where he spent a good part of his youth. For Haggard is, in a way, a distant soul cousin of Woody Guthrie, the radical dust-bowl poet who came from the same Okie background—in fact from the same area—southeast Oklahoma—from which Haggard's folks fled when the Depression hit bottom in 1935.

Guthrie's gut-level radicalism grew directly from the desperate circumstances of his people, but despite all that, there was a stubborn, it's-my-country-too kind of patriotism that was subtly embedded in songs like "This Land Is Your Land." Haggard came along a generation later. He could remember the desperate times, but he also knew that they were on the wane, and his music swung like a pendulum between those two realities.

His breast-beating patriotism stirred the crowds, and well it should have. But it never could obliterate a sense of being in it together with the traditional victims of America's failings—a feeling he captured with stunning, apolitical eloquence a little while back with a song called "White Man Singing the Blues."

> **The old man paid no mind to color**
> **'Cause he knew that I'd been down and out**
> **Old Joe said that I was a soul brother**
> **From things I'd been singin' about**
> **On the same side of the railroad track**
> **Where people have nothing to lose**
> **I'm the son of a gambler whose luck never came**
> **And a white man singing the blues ©**

It is not the only time Haggard has addressed himself humanely to the issue of race, which historically has been *the* issue for thousands, and perhaps even millions, of country music fans. Even more strikingly, for example, he released in 1974 a song called "Irma Jackson," which deals explicitly with one of the biggest taboos of them all—interracial love—and vehemently condemns society's lack of color blindness. "Of all the songs I've written," he says, "this one may be my favorite because it tells it like it is. I wrote and recorded it some time ago, but didn't release it for one reason or another, possibly because the time wasn't right. But I feel it's right now."

Whether it is or not is difficult to prove. For one thing, "Irma Jackson" was never released as a single, so its marketability on its own was never tested. But there are other people in the country-music field who share Haggard's opinion that times have changed, and one of those who shares it most passionately is a Nashville songwriter named Bobby Braddock.

Braddock is a quiet and unimposing reconstructed Southerner with faded jeans, a scraggly beard, and high and noble hopes for the future of his homeland. Professionally, he doesn't venture very often into the world of social commentary. Probably the most famous song he has ever written is the Tammy Wynette hit "D-I-V-O-R-C-E," which is best known to non-country music fans as the record an angry Jack Nicholson flung across the room in the movie *Five Easy Pieces*. Braddock is one of those gut-level, and sometimes hard-core, country writers whose work has been on the charts pretty consistently for the last half a decade.

In 1974, however, Braddock wrote a song that is a little bit different from his usual fare. For one thing, it flopped. At least the Bobby Goldsboro single on it did. But it is one of those engaging message-of-hope songs that has attracted the attention of a wide array of artists. Among those who have recorded it, in addition to Goldsboro, are Tanya Tucker, the teenage country idol whose diverse following has more than its share of bib-and-overalls Grand Ole Opry types, and Mariane Love, a talented, up-and-coming vocal stylist, who is black, beautiful, and a singer of the blues.

The song that all these people found it possible to identify with and that eventually became a top-twenty hit for Tanya Tucker is called "I Believe the South Is Gonna Rise Again," and this is the way Braddock tells it:

> **Our neighbors in the big house called us "redneck"**
> **Cause we lived in a poor sharecropper shack.**
> **The Jacksons down the road were poor like we were**
> **But our skin was white and theirs was black**
>
> **But I believe the South is gonna rise again**
> **And not the way we thought it would back then**
> **I mean everybody hand in hand...**
>
> **A brand new breeze is blowing across the Southland...**
> **And I see a brand new kind of brotherhood** ©

Such visions are fairly new to Bobby Braddock. He is not, in fact, the son of a sharecropper. On the contrary, his father was a citrus grower in central Florida, and Braddock grew up believing the things that the sons of modest privilege are supposed to believe in his part of the country. It wasn't that he consciously hated anybody, but he was unsympathetic to the changes that were taking place around him, and as late as 1968 he voted for George Wallace for president.

Precisely what changed him he isn't sure. The My Lai massacre began to undermine his hawkish views on Vietnam, and about the same time he began to rethink his opinions on other subjects as well. But more than anything else, Braddock believes, it was simply a different day. There was a different feeling in the air, a kinder and more mellow milieu that made it easier for the basic redneck decency in his corner of the world to make its way to the top.

And though Braddock really didn't think about it much at the time, there was also the quiet example of his friend and fellow songwriter Don Wayne, who is regarded by almost everyone who knows him as one of the gentler spirits on the country music scene. Wayne *did* grow up pretty much like the rednecks in Braddock's song. He was the poorly educated son of a transplanted sharecropper who had migrated from rural Tennessee to the big city of Nashville, seeking refuge from the hard-time Depression days. Wayne says he has a lot of memories from his boyhood, and one of the clearest is of his mother cooking for eight kids and singing blues songs she had learned from black neighbors up the road.

Now in his forties, Wayne is a slight and slow-moving man with a shock of sandy-blond hair, a thin and easy smile, and an unusually quiet and introspective manner. He has been a songwriter for about fifteen years, producing a respectable amount of material for albums and six or eight big hit singles. The biggest of those, "Country Bumpkin," came in 1974 and, helped by Cal Smith's earthy-rich rendition, was named country music's Song of the Year.

Wayne, however, is philosophical about awards and commercial success, realizing that both are ephemeral and believing that some of his best songs have been some of his biggest flops. One of those, which was cut in the late sixties by a talented but still obscure session musician named Weldon Myrick, was a ballad called "The Family Way." It tells the story of Aunt Elly Mae Jones, a black midwife who helps a frightened little white boy come to grips with his mother's out-of-wedlock pregnancy. "Now don't be harboring bad thoughts at your mother," she says. "A human is a human and a saint's mighty hard to come by."

The song is fiction, but it comes directly from Don Wayne's experiences, and there is something almost primordial in the Southern-ness of it: the back-country anguish, the unmet puritanical ethic—and, of course, the wisdom of Aunt Elly Mae Jones.

Aunt Elly Mae was no doubt responsible for the wretched air play the song received, for she can be as disconcerting to a lot of blacks as she is to many whites. The only problem is that she is real. Her relationship to white people is flawed, of course—she gives a lot more than she gets, and even the gratitude is tainted paternalism and inequality. But she has been around as a dispenser of strength and a symbol of shared humanity ever since antebellum times. Don Wayne simply appreciates her a little more than most people do.

"I guess one thing I'm trying to say," he explains simply, "is that blacks and whites have always been able to get along better than most people thought, if only we'd take note of one basic fact: we're all human, and we're all in it together. I've long thought that one reason black music and white music are so much alike is that the people are. They have the same wants and needs, and I think a lot of people are finally coming to understand this."

Implicit proof of Wayne's point came in 1975 in the form of a hit record called "Mississippi, You're On My Mind." It was a haunting sense-of-place song in the tradition of John D. Loudermilk's "Abilene" or George Jones's "Memories of Us," but there were several peculiarities that made it distinctive.*

The first was that it was written by a young white Mississippi-bred draft dodger named Jesse Winchester, who fled to Canada during Vietnam and hadn't been home since. The second was that the biggest hit version was done by Stoney Edwards, a good country singer who happens to be black; and the third was that the song was a smash hit in Mississippi.

Whether the traditional fans of country music were familiar with all those facts is open to question. Quite possibly they weren't, but that's beside the point. For as the politicians were debating issues such as amnesty and civil rights, Jesse Winchester, Stoney Edwards and the people of Mississippi were conspiring to demonstrate a truth that's worth grabbing hold of—that the things people have in common are a lot simpler and yet go a lot deeper than all the swirling abstractions that divide them. Jesse Winchester doesn't try to say in his song whether Mississippi is a good place or a bad place. It's just his place, and he missed it.

* Sense-of-place songs abound in country music. Some others that have struck home in recent years include Linda Hargrove's "New York City Song," John Loudermilk's "Tobacco Road," and Joan Baez's rendition of "Sweet Sunny South." In addition the country rock group Brush Arbor recently came out with a medley consisting of the old Asa Martin hillbilly song "I'm Going Back to Alabama" and Lynard Skynard's rock hit "Sweet Home Alabama."

# 7

# LORETTA & THE PILL:
## The Changing Relationships Between Men & Women

**The feeling good comes easy now since I've got the Pill!***
—*Sung by Loretta Lynn*

Spirits were high and flowing freely at the Charlotte Motor Speedway one crisp autumn night in 1975, as Conway Twitty and Loretta Lynn belted out their hard-driving country hits before nearly fifteen thousand auto race fans. Twitty, the fifties rock 'n' roller who turned country in the sixties and found his niche, came on first, wearing his lemon-yellow suit, his hair combed straight back and his spangled guitar strap turning back the glare of the floodlights.

There was something almost perfect about the setting: the crowd, full of close-cropped hair styles and freshly sunburned faces, watching in rapt appreciation, shrieking in continual bursts of recognition as Twitty ran

As the role of women has changed in American society, those changes have affected country music—especially the songs of Loretta Lynn. (Photo courtesy MCA Records.)

Dolly Parton epitomizes the modern compatibility of feminity and independence. (Photo courtesy RCA Records and Tapes.)

through his earthy repertoire . . . some of it becoming so sexually explicit that almost nothing was left to the fans' imagination.

They loved it when he finally came to one of his biggest and bawdiest hits in recent years, a crescendo ballad called "You've Never Been This Far Before." There were rebel yells and catcalls that sounded as if they might have come from a high-school locker room as Twitty sang of "trembling fingers touching forbidden places." And yet, despite the reaction they produce, there is a serious, almost somber side to Twitty's songs—a sort of gut-level accuracy in his description of the guilt and confusion that often occur with early comminglings of love and sex.

"Yeah, it's explicit," he said in a gruff and hurried interview after the show, "and I caught a little flak for it. But I still think it's one of the best songs I ever wrote. It's real."

The reality stems from jumbled emotions that have always been there in abundance among the good ole boys that Twitty is singing to. There has always been the assumption that nice girls don't and real men do, which can become a problem if you lose your grip on impersonality. The changing attitudes and mores of recent years have been a source of liberation, but there is a lingering fear, a counterconsideration not easily shaken, that the Good Lord is up there methodically taking notes in indelible ink.

A big problem for the Lord, however, is that he has lost a potent ally in recent times: the fear of pregnancy has given way to the pill; and that change has thrown not only the country music audience, but nearly everyone else as well, into one of the most profound fits of turmoil in the history of modern times. The separation of sex from consequence is an unprecedented boost for the temptations of the here-and-now, and it creates options and releases thoughts and considerations that were carefully repressed in times gone by.

Release is not liberation, however, and with it comes a whole new set of problems that are chronicled with a kind of flawed and earthy eloquence in the lyrics of country music. Families are shaken, men and women are rethinking the whole range of their relationships, and Hugh Hefner's predictions about how much fun it would be when contraception became a habit sometimes have a hollow and simplistic ring in the cold light of morning.

A Grand Ole Opry singer named Jean Shepherd caught the feeling not long ago with a ballad called "Another Neon Night"—a sort of feminine echo of "Help Me Make It Through the Night"—in which a liberated country girl finds that her sexual forays have failed their larger purpose. The song was not as big a hit as Sammi Jo's "Tell Me a Lie," which dealt with the same theme. But nowhere in all of country music has the pain of colliding values been expressed with any more power.

> **The neon light plays a sad tune on the ceiling**
> **There's a bottle standing empty by the bed.**
> **Silent stars sing silent songs**
> **And not a word's been said**
> **But a page filled up with loneliness has just been read.**
>
> **You can call it sin, but it's hard to spend**
> **Too many nights alone**
> **And the road I'm on ain't leadin' me back home.**
> **The only sound I'm hearin' now**
> **Is the silence of my shame.**
> **There's someone lyin' next to me**
> **And I don't even know his name...** ©

Songs that explicit have become almost the dominant genre of country music, which must be an eyebrow raiser to the God-fearing fans of yesteryear. But so it goes in the modern South: Baptist churches as abundant as they ever were, but massage parlors coming on stronger and stronger as time goes by. And like porno movies, country music sex songs don't have to be artistic achievements in order to succeed.

Positive proof of that fact was offered a while back by a Nashville songwriter named Little David Wilkins, whose career refutes the idea that success and writing talent are necessarily connected. One of his first hits was a forty-five minute creation called "Not Tonight I've Got a Headache," which displays almost exactly as much subtlety and lyrical imagination as its title suggests. Wilkins came back a few months later with another Top Forty chart-buster called "Whoever Turned You On Forgot To Turn You Off," clumsily written (at one point rhyming the words "lost," "loss," and "off") and making no point except to affirm his own interest in another man's sex-crazed castoff.

Little David, of course, is not alone in riding inane, sexually explicit songs to the top of the charts. The list is endless: Mel Street's "This Ain't Just Another Lust Affair," in which the hero reassures the girl in his motel room that somewhere in her arms the feelin' turned to love; or Billy Jo Spears's female reversal of the theme, in which the whiny-voiced heroine is contending that "just because we are married don't mean we can't slip around;" or Gene Watson's bedside temptation of a virgin, in which he tells her to "leave if you'd rather not lose what you came with, but stay and you'll find this is where love begins."

Kris Kristofferson is usually given credit for opening the floodgates, though the chances are that he didn't have Little David Wilkins in mind when he did it. Songs like "Help Me Make It Through the Night" or "Me and Bobby McGee" obviously have a purpose beyond the titillating of fantasies and the padding of bank accounts. Kristofferson's preoccupation was loneliness, which, in the real world, can become painfully interwoven with sexuality.

Actually, Kristofferson was not the only one around Nashville to make that connection. It was true that he was a rebel, and one of the norms he flouted was the tee-hee taboo about saying what you mean. But as Kristofferson was rising to prominence in the late sixties and early seventies, more traditional singers like Dolly Parton and Loretta Lynn were also toughening up their acts and dealing with some pretty down-to-earth stuff.

It was 1969 when Dolly wrote "Down From Dover," about a country girl with an out-of-wedlock baby on the way and a lover who had gone; and earlier still, Loretta Lynn had written "Wings Upon Your Horns," about a young girl used by a leave-'em-crying lover ("When you first made love to me, I was your wife to be," and so on). There were disc jockeys who were offended by such frank language from a sweet and sturdy native of Butcher Hollow, Kentucky, but Loretta Lynn has sailed on through such controversy to become one of the most important country singers today— at least in part because she personifies the stirrings among a large and crucial segment of America's female population.

Hers has been, to say the least, an unlikely odyssey. She grew up in eastern Kentucky, a few miles south of Paintsville, in a one-room cabin where she shared a bed with four other children. It was coal country, a rugged and spectacular land where questions of survival were never very far from the surface.

Today the land and the people are scarred by too many losing battles against the whims and greed of distant corporations. But in Loretta's childhood, the spirit was different. The Depression came quietly, as the dogged menfolk scratched and battled, trying to draw crops from the coal-infested earth. At night they descended beneath it to work the graveyard shift in the mines, while the women stayed home to nurse the babies, wash the clothes, and read the Bible by the light of a candle.

Eventually the Van Lear Coal Company pulled out, leaving Butcher Hollow, as Loretta puts it, "not much more 'n a ghost town today." By then she had long since gone.

At the age of 13 she met Mooney Lynn (nicknamed in honor of a home-brewed mash) at a schoolhouse supper where he had decided to sample one of her pies. Unimpressed with her abilities as a cook, Mooney nevertheless struck up a relationship that led, a month later, to a proposal of marriage. Loretta's parents, Ted and Clara Webb, were singularly unimpressed with the whole idea, but youthful unions were not uncommon in that part of Kentucky, and before long the Webbs relented.

A few weeks later, Loretta and Mooney were off to nearby Chandler's Cabins for their bewildering teenage wedding night, and the following year, at the age of fourteen, Loretta gave birth to her first baby girl. Three more children had followed by the time she was eighteen and at first, she maintains, her naiveté was such that she didn't even know what was causing them. She was five months pregnant the first time around before she knew what was wrong.

After leaving Kentucky, Mooney and his bride made their way to Washington state, where the early years of the fifties were spent in a one-to-one war on poverty. Mooney hired on as a lumberman and Loretta supplemented the family income by picking strawberries in the migrant labor fields.

It was during that time that Mooney bought her a used guitar, and she spent her spare moments singing and picking and composing songs. As the fifties drew to a close, she made a record called "I'm a Honky Tonk Girl," and she and Mooney traveled the country in a beat-up Ford to promote it. Fifty thousand records later, her career began to take off and she found herself in Nashville.

The songs she wrote and sang drew their power from a number of sources, including the years in Washington where Loretta—like so many of her fans of today—had lived within the traditional expectations about a woman's place. But if her outlook had been unrebellious, she had also learned something basic back in the desperate warmth of a coal miner's cabin: a sturdy sense of self and self-preservation that she has carried with her ever since. And with her budding career setting off an implicit erosion of at least a part of her feminine dependence, a different kind of spirit—a sort of don't-tread-on-me undercurrent—began to show itself in her music.

One of the first examples of that feeling was a song she wrote herself called "Don't Come Home A'Drinkin' With Lovin' on Your Mind," a wife's-eye view of a hard-drinking husband that invariably strikes a responsive chord among the women in her audience. The Charlotte Motor Speedway audience in the fall of 1975 was no exception, and as the ladies cheered, the men responded in a different way—shouting good-natured taunts and propositions that Loretta fended off with an adept, tough-mouthed flirtatiousness, obviously enjoying every minute of it.

Later, as her bus rolled in for a follow-up concert in Greensboro, Loretta lounged back in her blue jeans, bare feet, and number thirteen football jersey to reflect on some of her songs. "A lot of women have lived it," she says of "Don't Come Home A'Drinkin'." "I guess a lot of men have too, and 'course men ain't the only ones who drink. But it's a real song—all of my songs deal with something that's real, and that's why a lot of 'em get to be number one."

Of all her number ones, however, the one the people scream loudest for wherever she goes is "The Pill," her million-selling smash of 1975, which concerns exactly what its title suggests, and concludes with this happy affirmation: "Feelin' good is easy now, 'cause I've got the pill."

Loretta actually recorded the song around 1970 but kept it under wraps, waiting for the times to catch up. They never quite did. The record was banned on a dozen radio stations, giving it an aura above and beyond that of a story line that was racy enough to begin with. The woman in the song is an oft-pregnant housewife who is telling her good-timing husband that she now has the pill and therefore two can play at 'most any game in town.

Even in the increasingly raw world of country music, it was a little too much to handle in some quarters, especially with such a point-blank title. And yet it seems at least plausible that the male deejays who banned it were put off by something else as well—by the song's explicit denunciation of the double standard.

> For several years, I've stayed
>     at home, while you had all the
>         fun,
> And every year that came by,
>     another baby's come...
>
> I'm tired of all your crowin'
>     'bout how you and your hens
>         play
> While holdin' a couple in my arms
>     and another's on the way.
> This chicken's done tore up her nest
>     and I'm ready to make a deal,
> And you can't afford to turn it
>     down,
>         'cause you know I've got the Pill.*

It may be corn-pone protest, but it's effective nevertheless, and it's not the first time that Loretta has tried it. Her best effort in that direction came a few years earlier, when a brilliant satirical writer named Shel Silverstein penned a song especially for her. It was a hard-hitting ballad called "One's On the Way," and to a certain segment of feminine society it said far more than a hundred issues of *Ms.* or a year's worth of speeches by Gloria Steinem:

> Now what was I doin'?
> Jimmy get away from there,
> Darn, there goes the phone.
> Hello honey, what's that you say?

* Used by permission. All rights reserved. "The Pill" by Lorene Allen, T. D. Bayless, and Don McHan. Copyright © 1973 Coal Miners Music, Inc.

You're bringin' a few ole army buddies home?
You're calling from a bar?
Get away from there.
No, not you honey, I was talking to the baby,
Wait a minute honey the doorbell.
Honey, could you stop at the market and...hello,
Hello, well I'll be...

The girls in New York City, they all march for women's lib
And Better Homes and Gardens shows the modern way to live
And the pill may change the world tomorrow, but meanwhile today
Here in Topeka
The flies are abuzzin'.
The dog is abarkin' and
The floor need a scrubbin'.
One needs a spankin' and
One needs a huggin'
And one's on the way.*

Loretta laughs and grins a little uneasily when you ask her if maybe she hasn't just sung a protest song. Her own views, like those of many of the people who listen to her, are slowly evolving. But it's an unself-conscious evolution, unaffected by rhetoric or ideology. Movements are not her style. On the other hand, neither is dodging questions, and after a few moments she says:

"I sing about the things people go through, and 'One's On the Way' is something a lot of women experience. I think it's trying to tell men, 'I may not be a women's libber, but this is how it is, and it's not right.' Women sit at home and they see the television shows, and the soap operas, and they know their own lives are not what they oughta be.

"I'm not no libber," she says with her perpetual grin. "But women have got to stick up for themselves. If they don't, ain't nobody gonna stick up for 'em. A marriage ought to be fifty-fifty, and most of 'em aren't. Mine isn't. A lot of women that don't go in for women's lib are starting to take up for themselves, and I think that's good.

"Men don't have to be threatened by that. But you know," she says, dropping her smile for a moment, "I think a lot of them are."

* "One's on the Way (Here in Topeka)" Words and Music by Shel Silverstein. © Copyright 1971 Evil Eye Music, Inc. Used by permission.

The music on the men's side of the spectrum bears her out, at least in spots. There's been a lot of changes in the world since September of 1968, when Tammy Wynette recorded "Stand By Your Man" and watched it develop a fierce popularity—not so much among men as among women. But the sense of duty has eroded noticeably in the years following, and for men who are unsettled by that reality and looking for reassurance, there is the message of Johnny Paycheck.

Paycheck had made a career on innocuous songs of love gone sour. But he turned polemical in the fall of 1975 with a record called "All American Man," one of the most mean-spirited diatribes to come out of Nashville in the last ten years. It goes far beyond the standard (and fairly harmless) "Ramblin' Man" macho of people like Waylon Jennings, and what's more, Paycheck seems to believe it.

"All you men out there, you gonna love this song," he says in a husky-voiced intro that sounds as if he's gearing up for a bar fight. "And about eighty percent of you women, you gonna love it too. But for the twenty percent that don't like it, we wrote it just for you, darlin'."

What he wrote is really pretty startling in the latter half of the seventies, but there isn't much way to miss the point. There are put-downs of women who work, who in fact do anything but marry and make love, and the bottom line is this: "American woman, why can't you agree? God made man for himself, but he made you for me."

Of course, the basic message—that women are here for men to use—lurks behind the lyrics of a number of country songs, just as it lurks in the psyches of those who listen. "Billy, please get me a woman, I'm tired, and I feel so alone," sings Joe Stampley in a lonesome-truck-driver ballad. And as the song progresses, it becomes clear from the truck driver's specifications that almost any woman will do, as long as she doesn't make any demands for the future.

Whatever flaws of perspective the song may exhibit, however, it and most others like it lack the caprice of Paycheck's record. There is something sad and real in the feeling, a sort of masculine vulnerability that is there in stark and overstated terms in nearly every song that Conway Twitty and the rest of them ever do. And you have the feeling as the good ole boys in the crowd whistle and guffaw and slap one another on the back that the frivolity is tinged with overcompensation—with a kind of communal understanding that everybody's been there, and it's a hell of a lot easier if you can somehow bury the feelings. But you can't, of course, and the record companies know it, and the songwriters feel it, and it's one of the things that makes Nashville unique and irreplaceable.

Obviously there are Nashville writers whose views about all of this are frankly commercial. They know what will sell, and they churn out the songs, two a day, chuckling to themselves all the way to the bank. But I think the cynics are in the minority. For one thing, there can be few people who feel the pain of changing values more than some picker-poet out on the road and growing old fast, while the groupies tempt him and his wife waits at home—maybe. About the only good thing about that scene for him is that the times and the FCC will let him say things now that he couldn't say before. And so you have songs like Guy Clark's "Instant Coffee Blues," in which a lonesome lady and a road-weary traveling man are grappling, on more or less equal terms, with the emptiness that comes on the morning after:

> **He washed all the road dirt from his face**
> **and from his neck**
> **And sat down at her table and she picked**
> **up his check**
> **And she took him home for reasons that**
> **she did not understand**
> **And him he had the answers but did not**
> **play his hand**
> **For him he knew the taste of this wine**
> **very well**
> **It all goes down so easy but the next day**
> **is hell** ©

There is, of course, a happier side to country sex, and you find it in the gentle love ballads of people like Don Williams, a lanky Texan who can sing with understated power about relationships that work. But the dominant theme is pathos, and what emerges is a picture of men who are uneasy not only with the more assertive stance of women in the seventies, but also with the kinds of casual and easy encounters that should have been the dream of every red-blooded good ole boy between Georgia and California.

And so you have songs like Bill Anderson's "Somewhere Between Lust and Sitting Home Watching TV," which must be a gut-rocker to every suburban husband whose eye has ever wandered; or the Mel Tillis hit called "Woman In the Back Of My Mind," about a happily married man wrestling with the love that lingers from a relationship long since severed; or Tom T. Hall's poignant ballad about a Cub Scout daddy who knows his mistress is waiting at a cheap hotel.

People live all of that, of course, and if country music is too riddled with contradiction to put it all in place, it can at least help them sweat out the pain. "How I love that hurtin' music," wails Hank Williams, Jr., "'cause, Lord, I'm hurtin' too."

# 8

# GOD, THE GOSPEL, & COUNTRY MUSIC

**She stares at her coffee**
    **and looks toward the ceiling**
**But Lord, it's a strange place to pray**
    **at two in the morning on Saturday night**
    **at Rosalie's Good Eats Cafe ©**
              *—Shel Silverstein*

It was a wilting July weekend in South Carolina, just outside the booming little town of Rock Hill. The crowd of more than ten thousand had begun arriving early in the week; there were farmers and plumbers and preachers and salesmen, the hard-core folk from the back country, settling in at the Carowinds Amphitheater for a reverent, week-long festival of gospel music.

Some of the biggest names in the business were there—groups like the

114

The influence of religion is deeply imbedded in country music, and in the region in which the music was spawned. (Photo by Steve Perille.)

Preacher Will D. Campbell has
become a brother-confessor to
the rebellious musicians of
Nashville—drawing inspiration
from their songs, and helping,
in return, to keep them sane.
(Photo by Penny Weaver.)

LeFevres, the Kingsmen, and Coy Cook and the Premiers. And while it may be true that none of them would produce much awe outside of gospel circles, for the avid and the faithful it was roughly equivalent to seeing Elvis Presley, Elton John, and one or two of the Beatles all in the same week.

"It's entertainment and it's inspiration," explained Harold Pigford, a strapping South Carolina fan with sweat beads popping out on his sun-reddened forehead. "We go to shows like this whenever we can."

For Pigford and thousands like him the appeal of gospel music is simple and direct. Its message is unfailingly reassuring—an optimistic New Testament fundamentalism, nearly devoid of fire and brimstone terror, with Jesus the omnipresent soother of everyday travail. "My boat shall sail safely though the waves splash high," the LeFevres sing onstage, belting it out with a kind of high-pitched, hard-driving harmony that sets hands to clapping and shoes to tapping.

All of it is backed by the warbling melodrama of country steel guitars, and faint smiles of mellow satisfaction settle on the work-lined faces in the crowd. Even the restless, berry-brown children, tugging at the strings of their Carowinds balloons, can't quite tear themselves away.

"It's a time when people find themselves getting back to the basics," says Jim Hamill, settling his two-hundred-plus pounds into a padded backstage chair, as the sweat trickled down from his close-cropped sideburns. "I think people are tired of put-ons and con jobs, and I'm talking about the whole overall picture, the feeling, the vibes you sometimes get in this country. I think people want something real, and that's what this is— pure gospel."

Hamill, a gruff and sincere musician from the foothills town of Hendersonville, North Carolina, is the lead singer for the Kingsmen, an Asheville group that won one of gospel music's top awards in 1974 for its song, "When I Wake Up To Sleep No More."

He is heartened, he says, by the growing commercial success of gospel music, and he attributes it to the fact that most Americans, beleaguered as they have been by problems ranging from war to Watergate, are searching for escape. He admits, of course, that there is a simpler factor as well: The people who listen to him most—the sturdy churchgoers of Bonifay, Florida, or Dalton, Georgia, or Cookville, Tennessee—have been the beneficiaries in recent decades of the inexorable, amoebalike expansion of the American middle class. They have more money now to spend on records.

But Hamill also believes that the influence of gospel music (and by extension, the Gospel itself) has grown steadily, even as the world around it has become increasingly secular in its apparent preoccupations. As evidence he cites the long-standing, undiminished and perhaps even growing influence of gospel assumptions on the larger and less particularized field of country music.

There is scarcely a country singer who hasn't dabbled in gospel music at least upon occasion, and that includes even some of the most modern and rebellious. Kris Kristofferson's "Why Me, Lord?" was by far the biggest hit he ever had, lingering on the *Billboard* charts for nearly a full year—which makes it one of the most durable and successful songs in the history of country music. And yet such spectacular success is really nothing new. Roy Acuff's career was going nowhere fast until he stumbled upon "The Great Speckled Bird," and one of Hank Williams's most famous songs was the gospel classic, "I Saw the Light," written on a dismal Alabama highway just outside Montgomery.

But the link between gospel and country goes even deeper than songs dealing directly with the discovery of Jesus. There is often a religious factor in even the more earthbound country ballads (and most, of course, are emphatically immersed in the here-and-now). Sometimes you have to peel away the layers of meaning in order to find it, searching out the substance between the lines. At other times it's far more obvious, with an acute sense of the Lord and his expectations lurking unapologetically near the surface. Bill Anderson, for example, handled the link graphically a few years back, when he wrote "The Lord Knows I'm Drinking," a Top Ten hit detailing the sins and remorse of a high-stepping good ole boy who plans to have a heart-to-heart with God after one final round and a quick whirl with adultery.

Anderson's song was recorded and carried to prominence by Cal Smith, a veteran balladeer whose twangy-rich baritone gives a distinctive stamp to nearly anything he sings. But the most striking aspect of Smith's career, at least in recent years, has been his choice of material. Almost all the songs he has released have had some kind of theological dimension interwoven, often with considerable skill, into stories about the day-to-day existence of people on earth.

Perhaps the best-known example of that genre came in 1974, when Smith recorded "Country Bumpkin," the tear-jerking story of a gutsy barmaid with a gift for looking life straight in the eye. During the course of the song, the barmaid meets and marries a hayseed yokel, bears his children, and then "forty years of hard work later," dies—assuring husband and son before she goes that she will, in fact, see them later. The melodramatic story line escapes being maudlin by the finesse with which it was written, and somehow evokes a simple eschatology, a concern with ultimate destinies on earth and beyond that apparently got beneath the skin of the half million people who bought the record.

The target audience, of course, was hard-core country, and the theology simple and fundamental. There was a kind of cosmic optimism, a sunny and rocklike faith not only in the omnipotence of God, but in the certainty of a rosy future somewhere beyond the grave. Earthly optimism, on the other hand, was harder to come by, since life was never very easy or kind in the spawning grounds of the gospel tradition. Throughout the hollows of southern Appalachia, and the nooks and crannies of the deeper South, the obscure Calvinist sects—the Nazarenes, Pentecostals, and all the rest—grappled with the same assumptions that underlay the Negro spirituals of the nineteenth century: that life was what it was, and the future was frozen, and things wouldn't improve until the coming of the chariot.

"This world is not my home," they would sing, their a cappella voices taking on a power and a promise that would rattle the rafters, as the echo faded in the woods outside. But in the end, the hillbillies were wrong—at least their vision became a little fuzzy when they tried to peer into future generations, for things have changed in the rural South. The economy has become more benign, and against that backdrop, the righteous certainty of old-fashioned gospel can shade unconsciously into a kind of modern-day smugness. The feeling is somehow different when the faithful arrive in Oldsmobiles.

Perhaps for that reason, a new and more humble gospel influence is emerging from a handful of talented young writers, most of them from Nashville. In Mickey Newbury's "Lead On," or Larry Gatlin's "Help Me," there is an implicit understanding that worldly pleasures and treasures are attainable, for both Newbury and Gatlin have experienced their share. But there is still a yearning and a sense of inadequacy, stemming not as it once did from the austerity of the present, but from the empty feelings that linger even after a thorough and conscientious sampling of the things the world has to offer.

Some of the best writers in Nashville have tried their hand at that theme, but none have succeeded any more simply or eloquently than Dolly Parton, who was voted country music's top female vocalist in 1975 and who, by her own admission, has lived the contradiction between the lures and limitations of earthly pursuits.

She was born and raised in a rough-hewn cabin near the foothills town of Sevierville, Tennessee. There were twelve children, three of them older, reared by sturdy and moralistic parents, pillars of the local Church of God. The old farmplace yielded a reluctant living in the post-Depression forties, and Dolly can remember her share of nights without supper. But for the most part, she says, time has sweetened her recollections, and the things that stand out now are more idyllic—like Sunday School, and fireflies, and stolen kisses on the front-porch swing.

But girlhood was also a restless time. She hated school, loved to sing, and at the age of eighteen, with fantasies dancing in her brain, she struck out on her own for the big city of Nashville. She didn't know anyone when she arrived, and in the early years the loneliness took its toll. But she received some early encouragement from Chet Atkins and Bob Ferguson of RCA, and three years later, in 1967, she signed on as the better half of the singing duo of Porter 'n' Dolly.

She had a pure and spine-tingling voice, and a writer's gift for word pictures, but there was also what she described as "my gaudy appearance and overexaggerated features"—that is to say, the mound of blond hair that is not her own, and her awe-inspiring figure, which definitely is. Because of that veneer, it is only within the last few years that anyone outside a commited and longtime country following has bothered to take her very seriously.

But the message has gradually spread, and with people like Linda Ronstadt and Emmylou Harris recording her songs and *Rolling Stone,*

wander down to Old Town for an after-hours visit to the club where Prine was playing. "By the time we got there, Old Town was nothing but empty streets and dark windows," Kristofferson remembers. "And the club was closing. But the owner let us come in, pulled some chairs off a couple of tables, and John unpacked his guitar and got back up to sing.

"There are few things as depressing to look at as a bunch of chairs upside down on the tables of an empty old tavern, and there was that awkward moment, us sitting there like 'Okay, kid, show us what you got,' and him standing up there alone, looking down at his guitar like 'What the hell are we doing here, buddy?' Then he started singing, and by the end of the first line we knew we were hearing something else. It must've been like stumbling onto Dylan when he first busted onto the Village scene . . . one of those rare, great times when it all seems worth it."

Prine's selections that night were rough and gut-rocking creations—songs like "Donald and Lydia," about the lonesome, desperate fantasies of a fat girl and her would-be GI lover; or "Hello In There," the haunting story of two old people whose lives were slowly ebbing away. But perhaps the strongest song of all—and certainly the one that captured most thoroughly the Christian underpinnings of country compassion—was a bitter ballad called "Sam Stone." It tells of a broken, strung-out Vietnam veteran who meets his end in an overdose, and leaves a wife and kids behind him. It's an angry, disillusioned song that goes in part like this:

> **There's a hole in daddy's arm**
> **Where all the money goes**
> **And Jesus Christ died for nothing**
> **I suppose** ©

For reasons that had more to do with image than music, Prine has not gained widespread acceptance among the deejays who decide what the country music audience will and will not be permitted to hear. It's been a genuine loss, but because of the pressure of Kris Kristofferson, Tom T. Hall, Shel Silverstein, Johnny Cash, and a few dozen more, the early seventies were, nevertheless, a watershed era for strong country music.

Interspersed among the usual commercial pap were countless songs of hope and tragedy—of human, hard-living people grappling with nearly everything life can throw at you. There were songs of soldiers and winos, streetsingers and prostitutes, divorced daddies and homesick drifters, prodigal sons and unwed mothers. And there was even a Shel Silverstein opus entitled "Rosalie's Good Eats Cafe," which managed in the course of eight soul-racking minutes to be about nearly all of those things.

Many people believe it was the consummate achievement for Silverstein, a onetime *Playboy* cartoonist who began to dabble in country songwriting for the same reason he does nearly anything else: as he puts it, "to live an interesting life." It didn't take him long to master the art, for he has a remarkable mind hidden away in his clean-shaven head, and an uncanny eye for cultural detail.

The latter talent was never more evident than in his description of life after midnight in Rosalie's greasy-spoon diner—a setting he used as a kind of Chaucerian framework device for portraying the real-life problems of people. Every verse describes a different kind of tragedy, a different brand of poignancy; and by the time you finish listening to Bobby Bare's soulful rendition, you can't help but understand the Larry Gatlin theory of creative sadness.

This is the way Silverstein tells it:

> It's two in the morning on Saturday night, at Rosalie's
> Good Eats Cafe. The onions are frying, the neon is bright
> and the juke box is startin' to play. And the sign on the
> wall says "In God We Trust—All Others Have To Pay,"
> and it's two in the morning on Saturday night,
> at Rosalie's Good Eats Cafe...
>
> There's a tall skinny girl in a booth in the back, wearing jeans
> and a second-hand fur. She's been to the doctor and called up
> a man, and now wonders just where she can turn. She stares
> at her coffee and looks toward the ceiling, but Lord, it's a
> strange place to pray—at two in the morning, on Saturday night
> at Rosalie's Good Eats Cafe...
>
> Now there's an old dollar bill in the frame on the wall,
> The first one that Rose ever made; it was once worth a dollar
> a long time ago, but like Rose it's startin' to fade

**She's back of the register dreamin' of someone, and how things'd
be if he'd stayed. But it's two in the morning on Saturday night
at Rosalie's Good Eats Cafe...**

**The stoop-shouldered man and his frizzy-haired woman, it's
strange how their eyes never meet. He's playing the pinball,
she's fixin' the blanket of the baby asleep on the seat.
He's out of work, she's puttin' on weight; and they never
did have too much to say. It's two in the morning,
on Saturday night.
at Rosalie's Good Eats Cafe...***

I don't know if songs like that are religious or not. But I do agree with
Gatlin and a host of other songwriters around Nashville who argue that
people don't write that way if they have a cynical view of the human
condition. They don't often think such thoughts, or feel such compassion,
unless they believe deep down that life is more than a meaningless
accident. And that belief, many theologians maintain, is the distilled
essence of faith—the fundamental affirmation, not subject to proof or
logic, that everybody either makes or doesn't make sometime during the
course of his life. It seems to me that the affirmations of people like
Silverstein, Prine, Kristofferson, and Gatlin are pretty unmistakable.

That is not to say, of course, that the affirmations are conscious or
conceived in these terms. In most cases I am sure they are not, for
songwriters as a group are not given to cerebral ramblings. They write
from the gut or the heart, but certainly not from the head, and in fact for
the most part they are not even very righteous. How could they be? Their
lives are energized and bounded by things like speed and whiskey and
groupies and ego; the road and the one-night stands, the wild and
disorienting gyrations between obscurity and fame, and the treadmill
demands of piling hit upon hit to stay where you are. But intermingled with
all of this are what Mickey Newbury calls his "godlike thoughts," which
endure their earthly surroundings until they are put to music, emerging
finally as a sort of cosmic and universal expression of sadness,
compassion, or humble supplication.

It's a bewildering process, and all the more so if you are caught up within it. Which is why, I think, so many songwriters and related rebels around Nashville eventually make their way to the log-cabin porch of Will D. Campbell. Campbell is a peculiar fellow, a Baptist preacher and sometime songwriter who is about as comfortable as anyone I know with the contradictions of human nature. His religion tells him, with the help of the fifth chapter of Second Corinthians, that everybody is reconciled to God, and from there it's a minor metaphorical leap to a related conclusion: that there is no reason not to be reconciled to yourself. And so it's not the least bit surprising to Campbell that treasures come in earthen vessels, or powerful poetry from a troubled mind, or that a song about a prostitute could have religious dimensions.

Because of his serenity in the face of the world's bewildering juxtapositions, Campbell has become a sort of brother confessor to all sorts of people. He worked with civil rights leaders in the South during the fifties and sixties as a staff member with the National Council of Churches. Later, as director of an outfit called the Committee of Southern Churchmen, he established a ministry to draft resisters in Canada during the sixties and seventies, and informally, on his own time, he is a sort of spiritual advisor to a few dozen country musicians.

His relationship with the latter group is something unique. They will wander his way from time to time—Jessi Colter, Bobby Bare, Waylon Jennings, Kris Kristofferson, Vince Matthews, and all the rest—sometimes dragging their guitars along, and they will all sit around on his porch while Will cusses and spits and prays and sings their songs. Though the relationship may appear one-sided, it is not. Will may provide the musicians with perspective and help keep them from going completely crazy, but he gets his share in return. For Campbell is captivated by country music. He is fascinated by the relentless accuracy of its humanity, the implicit intermingling of joy and pain and God and sin; and he has made use of its insights in his chosen profession.

One day in 1969, for example, he journeyed to the little town of Granite Quarry, North Carolina, for a religious ceremony of sorts, one which in a way summarized both Campbell and the peculiar religiosity of country music. His purpose in going was to be with the family of Bob Jones, Grand Dragon of the Ku Klux Klan, on the night before Jones was to be shipped off to prison in Danbury, Connecticut. Campbell had developed a friendship with Jones that was odd in view of the philosophical gulf that separated them. But as a staunch believer in the gospel of reconciliation, he had grown to see the Klan as an alienated and troubled minority as much in need of his (or somebody's) ministry as draft resisters or civil rights protestors.

So he went to Granite Quarry, and it was a strangely festive occasion, with all the kinfolk and Klanfolk assembled in the living room of Jones's cinder-block home telling stories and trying to be jolly and unconcerned. The whiskey flowed and the laughter continued until about two in the morning, when Campbell proposed Communion. "Hell, yes," said Jones, "let's have Communion." So the people gathered in a circle, and Campbell unpacked his guitar, and said:

"I'm gonna sing a song that to me is the essence of the Christian faith. It's called 'Anna, I'm Takin' You Home,' and it's about a whore and a lover who forgives her and takes her home. That's what Christianity is all about—being forgiven and taken home to where you're loved." Then, strumming softly on his guitar, he began to pray.

"Lord, ole brother Bob is going off to jail for a while. We gonna ask you to kind of keep an eye on him. Lord, you know he's not a saint. And you also know that we sho ain't. But the Book tells us that's why you died. So that God and sinners could be reconciled. And we gon' drink to that, and if it's all the same, we gon' sing our song in Jesus' name:

"Anna, I'm takin' you home..."

So whether it's Will Campbell singing about a prostitute, or the Lefevres and the Kingsmen belting out a promise of life beyond the grave, country and gospel music speak to a wide variety of religious needs. Some are obvious, others are so unobvious that they are not even conceived as religious. But all are tied up with one thing that is, and always has been, the central preoccupation of country music: the human and imperfect grappling with the human and imperfect condition.

# 9

# PUTTING THE AUDIENCES BACK TOGETHER:
## Willie Nelson & the Austin Sound

The whole thing might have happened anyway, even if Willie Nelson's house hadn't burned, but probably not in the same way. For as the flames licked into the autumn Nashville night back in 1971, it was the low point in a decade of frustration for Nelson, a highly successful songwriter who always thought he could make it as a performer but could never persuade the bigwigs down on Music Row.

So as the flames crackled around him, he darted into the house, salvaged a pound of top-grade Colombian marijuana, and pointed his car in the direction of Texas. He had been born there back in 1933, in a little wind-swept town called Abbott. And like most expatriates from the dusty reaches of the Lone Star State, he had never quite gotten it out of his system—even when things were going well and he was writing classic country songs such as "Crazy," "Hello Walls," and "Ain't It Funny How Time Slips Away."

Nashville and Willie just hadn't been meant for each other somehow, and when he got back to Texas and began sorting things out, he caught the Lone Star fever again and decided to stay. Within a year of that decision, he found himself a kind of godfather figure in one of the most important developments, both musically and socially, in the latter-day evolution of rock and country music.

This development is the emergence in Texas of a musical form that goes by a variety of labels, "progressive country" and "redneck rock" among others. But whatever you choose to call it, it is essentially a fusion of rock and country sounds—and, more important, of rock and country audiences—that comes after a decade of polarization over everything from length of hair, to the color of skin, to the ardor of competing ideologies.

Slowly, in the last few years, the fusion presided over by Nelson and a handful of others has begun to spread, riding an impulse toward reconciliation and rippling westward in the direction of the Coast, then eastward toward cities like Charlotte, Atlanta, Nashville, and Philadelphia. The most tangible manifestations of the spread have been Willie Nelson's "Blue Eyes Crying In The Rain" and Michael Murphey's "Wildfire," a pair of hit singles that succeeded in both pop and country markets and between them have sold well over a million records.

But there are other manifestations as well: the rabid, packed-house followings of a hard-core country-rocker named Jerry Jeff Walker; the critical acclaim for the country-flavored big-band innovations of a group called Asleep At the Wheel; and the cult popularity of a new public television series, "Austin City Limits," featuring the cream of the Texas crop and, beginning in 1975, shown in 116 markets from coast to coast.

There is a kind of metaphorical logic in the fact that Austin, a bubbling college town and capital city of 300,000 people, would find itself at the center of the ripple. For Austin, says Michael Murphey, the gentle spirit and respected intellectual of the city's musical community, has always

The Austin Sound has exerted a crucial influence on country music of the Seventies, and Willie Nelson has become its godfather figure. (Photo by Melinda Wickman.)

A little of everybody gathers for a Willie Nelson concert. In the beginning that was the whole idea. (Photo by Melinda Wickman.)

Doug Sahm, a fiddle-playing prodigy in San Antonio's honky-tonks, became a mid-Sixties West Coast rock 'n' roller, then returned to Texas and country music. (Photo courtesy ABC Dot Records.)

Michael Murphey (left) and Jerry Jeff Walker embody the extremes of the Texas sound. Murphey is the gentle spirit, a soft-spoken intellectual caught up in the idealism of Austin's history. Walker is a charismatic country-rocker whose whoop-em-up lifestyle has become a Texas legend. (Photos courtesy Epic Records and *The Charlotte Observer.*)

One of Willie Nelson's most memorable performances came in 1975 at Ernest Tubb's Record Shop in Nashville. (Photo by Jim McGuire.)

With the possible exceptions of Kris Kristofferson or Mickey Newbury, Guy Clark may be the finest songwriter ever to come out of Texas. (Photo courtesy RCA Records and Tapes.)

been a place of natural fusions. It lies atop a geological imperfection called Balcone's Fault, which, according to the prevailing lay theorists in the area, is responsible for the area's peculiar topographical character.

Austin is the point at which the countryside begins to change dramatically no matter which way you go—quickly evolving into treeless, cattle-producing prairieland as you move north or west, drying up into cactus-covered desert country as you move south toward San Antonio and Mexico, and tangling itself into thick pinewoods and murky pockets of swampland as you move east toward Louisiana.

"And," says Murphey, "there is a social and musical analogy. You have the Chicano influence coming up from around San Antonio. You have a lot of blues and even some Cajun music spilling over from Louisiana, a pretty large jazz following associated with the university, and north of here country music is incredibly popular. Culturally, you have blacks, Chicanos, and a variety of European heritages. And overlaid across all of this, you have the cowboy culture.

"Austin," he concludes, "is the hub. It has a feeling of vitality that's pretty hard to match."

For the last forty years there have been people around Austin who felt that way, who appreciated talent for what it was and had the breadth of taste to revel in diversity. Chief among those people in the early years was a kindly old gentleman named Kenneth Threadgill, who transformed a filling station into a beer joint in 1933, and featured live entertainment once a week. Threadgill himself performed with the house band, a hard-country backup group that blended well with his Jimmie Rodgers style of yodeling.

But he also opened his stage to anyone who wanted to play there, and by the time the sixties rolled around, it was an exciting place indeed. One of the people who got her start there, for example, was an ex-coed from the University of Texas, a troubled, dynamic young woman named Janis Joplin, who went on to become one of the genuine, hard-living heroines of the West Coast rock culture.

Despite the efforts of people like Threadgill, however, things began to go a little sour in Austin, as they did nearly everywhere else in the late sixties and early seventies. In the wake of Cambodia, Vietnam, and Kent and Jackson State, the nation's mood began to darken, and Austin suffered as much as anyplace. More than some, in fact, for diverse and pluralistic cultures can become a hodgepodge of armed camps if you strip away the veneer of tolerance that prevails in happier times.

One of the people in Austin who understood all this, and had become deeply troubled by it during the early months of the seventies, was a bearded young lawyer and soft-spoken music buff named Mike Tolleson. Tolleson had become involved with a group of people who had opened a club and community center in August of 1970—a watering hole for freaks called the Armadillo World Headquarters, located in a spacious auditorium a few hundred yards from the Colorado River.

The Armadillo had blossomed out of a search for a congenial headquarters for the struggling but talented rock musicians who abounded in the Austin area and were resisting the usual migration to the West Coast. Eddie Wilson, manager of a group called Shiva's Headband, had happened to notice a vacant auditorium next door to a skating rink, and within a fairly short time he and some friends had transformed it into the Armadillo.

The beat of hard rock soon flourished inside its two-story walls, and the freaks poured in by the droves. The Armadillo people also developed a craft shop and practice room for musicians, and the stature of the place began to grow. But there was a disturbing thought in the back of their minds, a realization that, for the most part, only one type of person was apt to come to hear their music; and so they began to experiment a little. Among other things, they brought in the inventor of bluegrass, Bill Monroe, and some country-flavored freak rockers called the Flying Burrito Brothers.

Then, in the summer of 1972, they held their breath and took the biggest plunge yet—a leap back into the hard-core, honky-tonking past, with the west Texas beat of Willie Nelson.

"We thought if we could sell Willie to our audience, and bring in his old audience," remembers Mike Tolleson, draping his feet across the corner of his desk, "we could cross sectors and integrate these scenes culturally. That was something we really wanted to do because there had been a real sense of segregation in Austin, a pretty strong feeling of antagonism.

"We thought we could promote a kind of fusion and see different types of people come together so that Austin could be a total community. We also brought in Waylon, Tom T. Hall, and several others; and what emerged was a pretty different image—people became something more than just hippies, or just rednecks, and it was a very satisfying thing to see it happen."

Few people shared in the satisfaction any more emphatically than Nelson himself. For he is a rare figure in the country music scene—one of a handful of people (Kris Kristofferson is another) who produces more awe among those who know him well than among those who see him at a distance.

"It's really been an incredible thing," he said recently, thinking back over the last several years as he crumbled a pair of saltine crackers into a bowl of vegetable soup. Weary from a week on the road, Nelson had slipped away for a few minutes of conversation in the motel room of his longtime friend and drummer, Paul English. He seemed to savor the reflective minutes before the record company hangers-on and the giggling groupies with their pre-faded jeans and pointy-toed cowboy boots found out where he was and descended like flies.

"Yeah," he continued in the relaxed baritone voice that comes out with a twang when he puts it to music, "it was certainly a good thing. You had all these people who were afraid of each other, or thought they were, 'though I never quite saw it that way. I had played to enough different kinds of crowds to know they had more in common than they thought.

"But it's fun now. You can make a list of all kinds of people that come together at our shows, especially in Texas. Maybe if we keep putting on the shows, and if the same kind of crowds keep showing up, the time will come when nobody will have to make the lists anymore."

He smiles when he says it, and the smile does not go away altogether when his door bursts open and a record company secretary with a high-pitched voice and jeans that fit like a layer of skin asks if she and her friends can come in. The word has apparently spread, for the room quickly fills up with the faithful, and the serious conversation begins to dissipate.

Nelson is used to it, and accepts the inevitable with the kind of beatific resignation that has become his trademark. People say the serenity has always been a part of him, though that seems hard to believe if you look back on the early days when there were marriages that fell apart, and albums that didn't sell, and when the Music Row producers were telling him he was so good at writing songs that there was really no reason for him to try to sing them.

Now, of course, everything is different—especially in Texas, where the groupies, freaks, cowboys, and old people will travel for hundreds of miles and gather by the tens of thousands just to mingle in his presence. His Fourth of July musical picnics have become a semiofficial institution in Texas, with the 1976 outing drawing upwards of seventy thousand people.

"Down in Texas," concludes Waylon Jennings in gruff and sincere admiration, "they think that when they die they go to Willie's house."

To some observers, especially the rock-oriented journalists who are not yet hip to the sound of his music, Willie is a phenomenon that defies explanation. They point out—correctly—that his abilities as a picker, singer, and even a songwriter are not markedly more impressive than those of Texas colleagues whose names are less than legend. The question, then, is: Why Willie?

For starters, there's the fact that fads are contagious, and so is the excitement of a crowd that borders on being a mob. But still, there had to be a beginning point, and people like his drummer, Paul English, believe that Willie's meteoric rise is explained at least partially (and maybe even primarily) by the grinning serenity of his presence.

It's hard to say whether or not that's true, but there was certainly no evidence to the contrary one wintry evening not long ago when a fairly typical Willie Nelson crowd had assembled in frantic anticipation of his arrival. They endured the warm-up acts, then erupted into routine frenzy when he padded onto the stage wearing a T-shirt and tennis shoes, and carrying his battered Martin guitar.

He began to strum and then realized to his mild embarrassment that the guitar was out of tune. As he began the frustrating twang-twang process of trying to synchronize the strings, he leaned toward the microphone and asked good-naturedly, "How do you like me so far?" They cheered like maniacs.

Backstage when the show was over, Nelson, like any reasonable person, shied away from talking about auras—realizing that they are not much subject to precise dissection. But if serenity is the key intangible that combines with his music, he will let drop some hints about where it comes from. The hints, he says, are contained in his songs—which certainly seems to be the case.

Most of his tear-jerking jukebox ballads are distinctly autobiographical, as are the cuts from an obscure album called *Yesterday's Wine*, which came out in 1971 and can now be found in the two-dollar bins of sophisticated record stores. But if the album didn't sell very well, in Nelson's mind it is nevertheless the most potent and personal record he's ever produced.

It's an opera in a way, a sort of rough country equivalent of *Jesus Christ Superstar*—not so much in its content as in the originality of its approach. It's a concept album, tracing with unabashed theological overtones the ups and downs of a typical life, and revealing in the process a crucial fact about Willie Nelson—that despite his honky-tonking history and fast-paced present, he is about as deeply religious as anyone around.

The revelation is scattered throughout the album but probably is found most clearly in an uncomplicated song called "It's Not for Me To Understand." This gospel tune tells the story of a man walking past a yard full of children, one of whom is a little blind boy and standing alone and off to one side. The man, who is Nelson, is moved by the scene and demands to know how God could permit such a heart-breaking turn of events. The answer turns out to be this:

> **After all you're just a man**
> **And it's not for you to understand.**
> **It's not for you to reason why**
> **You, too, are blind without my eyes** ©

It's a frankly sentimental song, but the humility it contains is the profound and universal variety that comes, Nelson says, when religion sinks in deep. And it can provide, he adds, some pretty stout emotional armor against the vagaries and absurdities of everyday life.

In any event, whatever it was that gave Nelson his powers of endurance, his eventual stardom has proved an understandable inspiration to a host of

Texas pickers whose day has not yet arrived. And so he became the catalyst, the momentum began to grow, and almost overnight Austin filled up with a remarkably talented array of poets and musicians of every stripe.

The supply had been around for some time in the form of people like Rusty Wier, but the legions were beefed up considerably in the early seventies when Jerry Jeff Walker, Michael Murphey, Steve Fromholz, Doug Sahm, Townes Van Zandt, Bill Callery, and quite a few others moved in to stay.

Of all those mentioned, one of the most significant has turned out to be Sahm, who made it pretty big in the mid-to-late sixties as the lead singer for a British-style rock group caled the Sir Douglas Quintet. What the teenyboppers didn't know, however, and probably didn't want to know, was that Sahm and the quintet were products of the very un-English city of San Antonio, Texas.

He had grown up there in the forties and fifties—a fiddle-playing prodigy in the redneck honky-tonks, who also had a habit of wandering crosstown to the blues clubs, to share a stage with the likes of T-Bone Walker. But it was rock 'n' roll that finally took hold of Sahm's life during his high-school years, and after graduation he gathered together a quintet of rockers and headed for the Coast.

There was a string of mid-sixties hits, including "She's About a Mover" and "Mendicino," both of which were written by Sahm. But things grew quieter after that, until Sahm resurfaced in 1972 with a slap-happy solo album featuring a whole bunch of country songs and some able backup work by a musical compatriot named Bob Dylan.

Sahm had moved back to Texas by that time, settling in comfortably on the rock side of the country-rock spectrum, but getting countrier and countrier as time went by. He now lives in a cabin on the outskirts of Austin, nestled in among the scrub oaks a few hundred yards from a music hall hangout called the Soap Creek Saloon.

He agrees with little hesitation these days to talk about his musical odyssey (he prefers to call it a trip) and generally suggests the club as the site for discussion. It's an excellent choice, for the Soap Creek is a delightful place, congenial and easygoing with low ceilings, pool tables, and an adjacent 300-seat concert room that boasts a double-size fireplace.

The interview is set for late afternoon, and the club is inhabited only by a waitress and a couple of good ole boys who have been there long enough for the Lone Star beer to give way to a round of Tequila Sunrises. Against the wall an early-vintage Wurlitzer jukebox is standing idle, but next to it a more modern version loaded with Doug Sahm records is blaring forth with "Groover's Paradise," the title cut from a recent album.

The man himself strolls in after a few minutes, looking for all the world like the ageless Mr. Hippie. He's thirty-four years old, but you'd never be able to tell that by his T-shirt uniform, angular face, and shoulder-length hair, which is straight and getting on toward being unkempt.

He plops his slender frame into a chair near the bar and offers to let a pair of Eastern visitors finish their game of eight-ball before the conversation gets underway. But he seems obviously antsy and ready to get on with it, so the cue sticks are temporarily laid to rest and the pitcher of Lone Star is transported to his table.

It soon becomes apparent that interviewing Sahm without a tape recorder is a definite mistake. Asking a question is like flicking a switch, and the ideas spew out like champagne from a shook-up bottle—the syntax askew, the transitions nonexistent, but somewhere in there a nugget of understanding that holds your attention.

There was a point early in the conversation when he was asked, obviously enough, what brought him back to Austin. The answer came out something like this:

"Well, I was out there on that whole West Coast scene, man, you know, in San Francisco, that whole Grateful Dead trip, you know; it was getting pretty heavy, I don't know, it just kinda burned itself out . . . you know what I mean, like big cities, like what's happening in New York today, you know, so I just came back to Austin. People are still there, there are still jobs; and we got into the country thing, and our music now is countrier than ever. I can't 'splain it."

Or words to that effect.

The odd thing is that after a while it all seems to make sense, and what emerges is this: In Sahm's mind the big-city scene has basically turned bad, and there is some kind of analogy or connection between the bummed-out craziness of the Haight-Ashbury drug culture, the proliferating concrete of urban Los Angeles, and the teetering financial problems of New York City. In the face of those things, Sahm believes, a lot of people are heading back to less complicated places, and more specifically, in many cases they are heading home—back to the roots. That reality, he says, is one of the key energizing forces of the Austin musical movement.

Sahm runs through all of this, and once he has explained it to his satisfaction if not everyone else's, he sniffs and belches, slaps both hands on his thighs, and says abruptly: "Well, is that about it?" It turns out that it is, and he rises, shakes hands, and reaffirms his earlier declaration that he wants to do some gigs back east in places like North Carolina.

In back of him, the waitress, wearing a friendly smile and a Doug Sahm T-shirt, shakes her head in the perpetual amazement that Sahm seems to generate. "He's something else, isn't he?" she says with a laugh, and then launches into a monologue on the crowds that pour into the Soap Creek when Sir Doug performs.

"It's really weird," she says. "You get a little bit of everybody here. For a long time, it was a young, kinda freaky crowd. The older folks were a little scared of the place. The first year or so, there were some people who came out here that were into dealing drugs, but we've got that cleared up, and now it's a real mixture. The freaky ones still come, but so do some older, you know, straighter people. And there are a lot of people like in their twenties—late twenties—and thirties."

That in-between crowd is hard to define. They are not exactly freaks, and they don't look like rednecks—in fact, they seem to include a little bit of everybody.

Some are thirtyish onetime collegiate radicals who grew up as comfortable conservatives in places like Dallas or the dust-bowl towns farther west, then went away to school and found themselves permanently radicalized and temporarily alienated by the war and the upheavals of the last ten years.

They may have no more intention of giving up their politics than Sahm has of backing away entirely from rock 'n' roll. But over pitchers of beer in the country music clubs in downtown Austin, they will tell you they are fed up with the alienation and have come back to Texas because it's home.

They form part of the crowd, but there are also other types represented. There are the rednecks and good ole boys who are young enough to have been influenced by the turmoil of recent decades—not only the war, but the ethnic awakenings and the mind-numbing string of cultural fads from Beatlemania onward. Their hair may be a little bit longer, and their ideas a little bit different, but they are, as an up-and-coming singer named Milton Carroll put it, "your basic country audience."

"It's really a hell of a thing, man," says Carroll, who records for Willie Nelson's Lone Star label. "It's roots, you know what I mean? There ain't no way to change where you're from."

And if you can't change it, you may as well flaunt it, and they do a lot of that at places like the Castle Creek Club in downtown Austin. When Friday night rolls around, they will pour from the woodwork with their cowboy hats and faded denims—clapping and whooping like crazy people, while up on the stage Jerry Jeff Walker is blitzed as usual and leading a cast of his buddies through "Goodnight Irene" and "Will the Circle Be Unbroken?"

The applause and rebel yells will sometimes linger for a full five minutes after he is through, and he will return to the microphone, lurching forward with a grin, and say, "These are hongry people. They'll clap for anything."

But those scenes are not limited to Texas. Roughly the same thing happens, for example, when Jerry Jeff visits places like Charlotte, North Carolina, and it's a peculiar sight in a part of the country where the nearest real cowboy is a thousand miles away.

There are excesses in there someplace, and they can be disturbing to the grizzled Texans whose identity has never been much in doubt, and who are a little put off by the prospect of having their culture turned into something it isn't. And indeed if the dusty-boots trappings were all there were to it, the Austin sound would no doubt melt into the past as quickly as hula hoops, bomb shelters, and blue suede shoes.

But after five years, it shows no signs of melting and in fact is growing in popularity. The reason for that, of course, is that there is more to it. Beneath the shit-kicking exterior, there is a celebration of the humaneness that has always resided in the Texas culture, and nowhere is that fact illustrated more graphically than in the music of Guy Clark.

Clark is a decent, Sleepy-John type of fellow, who grew up in the western flatlands town of Monahans and then wound up in Nashville a few years back with a promising contract to write some songs. Although he no longer lives in Texas, he still performs there and writes from his boyhood there—from the days during World War II and afterward, when he was raised by an oil-drilling drifter named Jack Prigg.

Prigg was, as Clark puts it, "my grandmother's boyfriend," a tobacco-chewing, domino-playing old man whose life and death and friendship heightened in Clark an instinctive understanding that you find in the most poetic songwriters—a realization that there are often hopeful, and even inspiring qualities in the saddest and most tawdry of circumstances. In the course of his thirty-five years, Clark has genuinely befriended all sorts of people, from winos, to hitchhikers, to prostitutes, and his music as a result is shot through with a kind of rough-hewn sympathy and sensitivity.

Probably the best example of all that is the song he wrote about Prigg, which goes in part like this:

> I'd play the Red River Valley
> And he'd sit in the kitchen and cry
> And run his fingers through 70 years of livin'
> And wonder Lord, has every well I drilled run dry
> We was friends me and this old man
> Like desperados waiting for the train
>
> He's a drifter and a driller of oil wells
> And an old school man of the world
> He taught me how to drive his car when he's too drunk to
> And he'd wink and give me money for the girls
> And our lives was like some old western movie
> Like desperados waiting for the train
>
> The day before he died I went to see him
> I was grown and he was almost gone
> So we just closed our eyes and dreamed us up a kitchen
> And sang another verse of that old song
> Come on Jack, that son of a bitch is coming
> And we're desperados waiting for the train ©

Although the scenery of the song is taken from Texas, the feelings behind it are too universal to be confined to a region. The same is true of much of the other music coming out of Austin, and as a result the fans are multiplying throughout the country.

A lot of them are young, like the five thousand or so Vanderbilt University students who turned out for Clark and Willie Nelson not long ago and grabbed hold of country music as if it had been invented especially for them. There were people around Nashville who grumbled, after that, that Willie had turned his back on country music's traditional fans, and Roy Acuff even said as much on the stage of the Grand Ole Opry.

But the theory came tumbling down a few weeks later when Nelson was invited to appear at the Midnight Jamboree at Ernest Tubbs's Record Shop. As it turned out, it was a performance that underscored as clearly as any other the symbolism of the Texas movement.

For Ernest Tubbs's is a funky place. Its Jamborees every Saturday night now draw the stalwarts who have never quite adjusted to the fact that the Grand Ole Opry has gone uptown. They are the hard-core folk who still pour in from the hinterlands in their pickups and workday khakis to revel in the music of white man's soul.

But when Nelson appeared back in mid-October, the crowd was a little bit different. It contained, in addition to its regulars, a smattering of Nelson's newer and shaggier fans, and there were discreet murmurs in various parts of the room about why the hippies were there. Some of the murmurs, in fact, were directed toward Nelson himself, as he made his way through the throng, prominently displaying his flaming red beard and a blue-checkered bandanna looped around his shoulder-length hair.

But when he finally made it to the stage and began to sing, the audience's mood changed abruptly: they whooped and screamed and wouldn't let him leave. In the back of the crowd, the whole event was summed up pretty eloquently by an ole boy with close-cropped hair and a round, perpetually flushed face.

"Yep," he said, rocking back and forth from heel to toe, as his voice took on an air of authority, "ole Willie'll be all right."

# 10

# SOUTHERN ROCK:
# The New Good Ole Boys

**The South's gonna do it again.**
—*Charlie Daniels*

A late winter's night in Nashville, and the city auditorium is jammed to the gills. Every high-school and college student within a hundred-mile radius appears to have migrated in for a concert by the Marshall Tucker Band. The atmosphere is giddy, and if it weren't for the wafting faint smell of burning marijuana, you'd swear the place had the feel of the midnight madness at Ernest Tubbs's.

Bass player Tommy Caldwell surveys the scene, flashes one of his patented grit-eating grins, and moves toward the microphone with a country boy's swagger. He still has some of that kick-over-the-barstool stage presence that he and the other Tuckers developed in the sleazy

Rock 'n' roll began as a Southern fusion of country and blues, and this is the man who's responsible. (Photo courtesy *The Charlotte Observer*.)

Elvis as a boy in Mississippi had little of the sultry intensity he would later display on stage. (Photo courtesy *The Charlotte Observer*.)

Nobody embodies the Southern fusion of country and rock any more than hard-living Charlie Daniels, shown here in a guest appearance on the Grand Ole Opry. (Photo courtesy CBS Records.)

The boys in the Marshall Tucker Band don't have the look of country musicians, but in 1976 their recording of "Long Hard Ride" was nominated for a Grammy as country instrumental of the year. (Photo courtesy Capricorn Records.)

southside clubs of Spartanburg, South Carolina—back in the days before the Tuckers had become, along with the Allman Brothers and The Charlie Daniels Band, the prime practitioners of Southern rock. But the days of dodging beer bottles and eking out a living are behind him now; the crowds are friendly and raucous, and Caldwell knows when he has them in his hand.

"We gon' do a song from our first album," he says, grabbing the mike stand and planting his feet as if he plans to be there awhile. "We got some guy that's gon' play fiddle with us from Nashville. Don't know if ya'll know who he is, but it looks like ole Charlie to me."

As the crowd erupts into war whoops and rebel yells out strolls Charlie Daniels, looking like a friendly, fiddle-playing grizzly bear, only bigger, his cowboy hat pulled low over his eyes and his fiddle bow cocked at the ready. With the amps turned up full blast, he and the Tuckers launch into the hard-rocking, country-flavored beat of "Fire on the Mountain"—the faithful surging toward the stage and crushing together like rebel sardines, the girls, often as not, perched on the shoulders of their shaggy-haired dates, clapping and swaying and calling for more.

It continues that way for about three hours, which is a pretty standard show these days when groups like the Marshall Tucker Band or Charlie Daniels and company are touring their native Southeast. And although frenzy has been a staple of rock 'n' roll camp followers ever since the early days of Elvis, there is somehow a difference in quality between the chemistry of today's Southern rockers and, say, the drug-cult, guitar-smashing antics of Kiss or Alice Cooper.

Southern rock, at its best, is something more than rock that happens to be played in the South, and its fans are reveling in something more than the sound of the music. They may not understand it fully, may not have sorted out all the pieces, but the people onstage understand it very well. They are people like George McCorkle, the affable, slow-talking rhythm guitarist for the Marshall Tucker Band, who finds himself, at the reflective age of thirty, intrigued by the substance of the music he's been involved in ever since he picked up a guitar.

"After a while," he says, sitting backstage before the show, his elbows propped on his knees, "you get older and your music matures. You start playing your roots—country, blues, or whatever. It's what you grew up with and you can't escape it."

That's the view of a lot of Southern rockers. They see their craft as a fusion of very old musical forms, with roots running from Smoky Mountain hillbilly pickin', to the crystal-clear notes of Florida bluegrass, to the sleazy blues bars that grew up in Memphis and New Orleans at the turn of the century. It's logical that it would be that way, for rock 'n' roll began as a distinctly Southern hybrid—an Elvis Presley/Carl Perkins kind of blend of black man's blues and white man's country.

In their early days, in fact, Perkins and Presley held on to their original audiences, with Perkins's "Blue Suede Shoes," for example, hitting the top of both country and rhythm and blues charts. Quickly, however, rock began to develop a more youthful audience of its own, and eventually, after a trip across the ocean and back, it struck out in assorted electrified directions that bore little resemblance to the point of origin.

Today's Southern rock—at least as practiced by the Marshall Tucker-Charlie Daniels-Allman Brothers clique—is essentially an attempt to recreate and refine some of the original fusions in a modern-day setting, turning loose all the amps and volume of the West Coast acid rockers, but blending in the craftsmanship of old-time blues and country.

It is no accident, the Southern rockers say, that all of this is happening at a time of peculiar goings-on in the South. For Southern music—whether blues, country, or barroom boogie—has always been a remarkable barometer of the society in which it thrives. And so it is today, as the South emerges from twenty years of turmoil, and the young people who were estranged from their region and heritage during the years of upheaval begin to realize that once a few key sins are purged, theirs will not, in fact, be a place to be ashamed of.

"Barriers have broken down between groups of people, just like between categories of music," affirms George McCorkle, making an instinctive, on-target connection between music and sociology. "Kids aren't ashamed of country anymore, and they're not ashamed of blues. And when you mix it all together and the music gets to cooking, it's a pretty damn exciting thing to be around."

The philosophizing jogs something in McCorkle's memory, and he lets loose a country boy's soliloquy on the early days in Spartanburg, and how even today he loves to go back and play country music or whatever he feels in the beer-spattered clubs where the whole trip began. "It's all what you grew up with," he says by way of concluding the conversation. "It's Southern."

With that he excuses himself politely and threads his way to the tuning room where Daniels and the rest of the band are belting out bluegrass harmonies to some straight and unamplified country picking.

He ducks inside, escaping a backstage chaos that rivals the scene in the auditorium itself. There are dozens of groupies, resplendent in faded jeans and braless T-shirts, including one that proclaims, in big block letters, "AIN'T IT GREAT TO BE ALIVE AND IN TENNESSEE." And in a sort of odd and homey counterpoint, there are also a goodly number of wives and children, licking their fingers and munching away on a tableful of barbecued ribs—mingling in the process with reporters and record company people who are putting away awesome quantities of Budweiser beer.

It's weird and dizzy, but it has, nevertheless, all the feel and fervor of an old-time family reunion.

The family headquarters these days is in the sleepy Southern outpost of Macon, Georgia. The city is, at first glance, the ideal sort of place to be from—a faded childhood memory of fried-chicken picnics and hand-cranked peach ice cream, all on a manicured lawn without ants. The gentility of the Old South rustles up and down the tree-shrouded streets like the first breeze of a July afternoon.

But the beat of the New South is becoming more and more prevalent, especially in a converted slaughterhouse over on Cotton Avenue. That particular slaughterhouse, along with the brownstone next door and a well-appointed studio just across town, are the home digs of Capricorn Records, one of the largest independent record producers in the world and the prime evangelist of Southern music. From this casual home base have flowed the frenetic, white-boy blues of the Allman Brothers and the down-home country funk of the Marshall Tucker Band, the hard-edged bar boogie of Wet Willie and the sweet Southern soul music of Otis Redding, all to the tune of some twenty-five million record albums in 1976 alone.

Capricorn Records, headed by a shrewd and chauvinistic Southerner named Phil Walden, has ramrodded the revival of Southern music into something of a national mania, leaving the sleepy streets of Macon littered with a few long-haired millionaires along the way.

"But this is not a new phenomenon," Walden insists, as he leans back in his overstuffed chair and surveys his eighteenth century broad-topped desk. "The music has always been here. The phenomenon is that it's being done down here. People—musicians—are remaining in Southern communities to record and perform. We've got a base here now."

The base was a long time in coming, for the South has always been slow and cautious in its flirtations with technology. But the music itself, like the other resources springing naturally from the land and its people, has been around for centuries—spreading inexorably from the point of creation to the eager consumers elsewhere in the land.

Walden maintains, in fact, that almost all of American music is traceable to the South, and he may be pretty close to right. From the simmering poverty of Appalachia came the eloquent statements of hillbilly music, eventually flowing down from the hills into a booming city called Nashville and a collapsing auditorium called the Ryman. From the Carolinas and the scrub palmetto flatlands of Florida, traditional Scotch and Irish folk music mutated (with the help of the Kentucky-bred influence of Bill Monroe, among others) into the mandolin wind known as bluegrass. In the urban melting pots of Memphis and New Orleans a whole new class of citizens— blacks fleeing the farms after the Civil War—found a world even more appalling and gave poignant voice to that world with the blues and, later, jazz.

Nor were the musical forms content to remain separate. In a society generally painted in hues of black and white, the music knew very little color. Jimmie Rodgers, the first hillbilly superstar, took both his guitar and his singing styles from the black railroad workers in Meridian, Mississippi, and is best remembered today for his yodeling interpretations of the blues. And on the other side of the line, Lillie Mae Glover, who sang the blues as Memphis Ma Rainey along Beale Street in the twenties, remembers that one of her most requested numbers was a hillbilly lament called "Heart Made of Stone." That song, she says, had soul.

The blues and hillbilly music came together once and for all one afternoon in 1954, when a small-time Memphis record producer named Sam Phillips and an unknown hillbilly singer named Elvis Presley decided to try something a little bit different. What they tried was infusing the black soul of the blues, with its overtly sexual imagery, into a harmless little hillbilly song sung by the former truck driver from Tupelo, Mississippi. What Phillips and Presley and ultimately, the rest of the world got was rock 'n' roll. The explosion that followed quite literally rocked the world, and Southern music, more than ever before, had gained widespread acceptance.

But there was more to come. Over in Nashville a couple of Kentucky-bred kids, Don and Phil Everly, came up with a song called "Bye Bye Love," written by the incredibly successful songwriting team of Boudleaux and Felice Bryant. The Bryants had already offered the song to more than thirty artists, including Porter Waggoner, but none had displayed much interest. In the hands of the Everlys, however, "Bye Bye Love" became a watershed hit, quickly soaring to number one on both the pop and country charts.

Meanwhile, equally potent forces were beginning to stir in slow-moving Macon. Over a sink full of dirty plates at the Greyhound Bus Station, a dishwasher named Little Richard was busy writing a song called "Tutti Frutti" and would soon do a little world-shaking of his own. And while Elvis, Little Richard, and the Everlys got ready to rock through the fifties, another black Macon singer by the name of James Brown was already laying the groundwork for the next great musical step—the modern-era soul music that would soon, ironically, make Detroit a recording center.

By the end of the musically frenetic decade of the fifties, another Macon figure was beginning to make himself felt, at least in a tentative way. A teenaged Phil Walden had wandered across the railroad tracks separating genteel Macon from the sleazy black beer clubs and the gritty black soul music and was soon managing a black band of his own.

But Walden's band kept being clobbered in local talent contests by yet another Macon soul singer—a fellow by the name of Otis Redding—and Walden, whose opportunistic streak had matured at an early age, decided to shift allegiances. He became Redding's manager, booking him into clubs and college auditoriums, and the two men were soon riding the crest of a soul music tidal wave. Walden and Associates rapidly attracted other soul acts, including Clarence Carter, Sam and Dave, Arthur Conley, and Percy Sledge, and the Macon offices were no longer quite so quaint or quite so far removed from the mainstream of music.

And the mainstream was about to take a quantum step closer to Macon. In 1969, Walden went to Muscle Shoals, Alabama, to hear a sessions musician named Duane Allman. Walden was impressed, and suggested that Allman get together a band and move to Macon. The rest is history. Duane Allman did exactly that, and Southern rock had come of age.

It's a sad sort of irony that the Allman Brothers Band developed a Hollywoodish image in the midseventies, thanks to the jet-set antics of Gregg Allman—his on-again-off-again marriage to Cher Bono and his prosecution testimony in the cocaine trial of the group's former manager. The Allmans split up in 1976. In the end the pace was just a little too fast, the living just a little too high, for a bunch of Southern kids who stuck it out on the home-front, touring incessantly and turning on the locals with a different kind of music.

But nothing could detract from the importance of the music. At the white-hot core of the Allmans' sound was the vital interplay between blues and country—a musical mirror of the central tension of Southern life, the interaction between black and white. Allman music at its best is a sometimes subtle, sometimes overpowering blend of black urban blues—in the vocals of Gregg Allman—and the bluegrassy strains of old-fashioned country—in the vocal and guitar work of Richard Betts—with just enough jazz and hard-edged rock 'n' roll to keep the whole mixture cooking.

Beneath Gregg Allman's electrified bar blues (and he has one of the finest white blues voices in the country), there's always the slightest hint of a bluegrass guitar, a tiny reminder that blue skies are just ahead. Beneath even the most folksy of Richard Betts's country compositions are the underlying pain and loneliness of the blues. And somewhere between the two poles of black and white, urban and rural, blues and country, lies the soul of Southern music.

There was a time, says Betts, who grew up picking bluegrass and listening to Hank Williams in the sun-blasted heartland of central Florida, when being from the South was anything but an asset to an aspiring rock 'n' roller. "For so long," he explains in his easy drawl, "the scene was either in England or in New York or LA. For so long, Southern groups had to copy that sound. The Allman Brothers were the first group to say, 'Fuck it, we're gonna stay in Macon.'

"It's really interesting," he continues. "People are starting to realize that Southern music is something really good that they've overlooked for a long time. It's not anything new. It's just being discovered. It's almost like a cultural thing started happening."

The cultural thing, he believes, was a Southern coming of age. The central tension may still be around, but there has been a profound, even radical reordering of the interplay between black and white. And it came at a time when the South was being hit with all the other mind-bending, homogenizing, fabric-tearing forces that were being unleashed in the country at large—from the proliferating influence of television to the bloody street battles over the war in Vietnam. Through it all, the South was changed. But it was not changed altogether, and that fact is underscored most graphically in the music and self-conscious Southernness of Tennessee's Charlie Daniels.

Daniels is not a Capricorn act (he's on the Epic label), but he cuts most of his records in Macon, and before a recent session he grabbed a few minutes to talk about his peculiar career.

It was morning, which is not exactly his favorite time of day, and he looked a little bleary around the eyes as he ambled into a vacant side office at the Capricorn studios. As he settled himself on the vinyl-covered couch, the belly snap popped on his cowboy shirt, displaying some ample padding about the midsection. He ignored the futile chore of resnapping, leaned back, and occasionally spit excess tobacco juice into a worn-out Styrofoam cup.

Daniels is widely thought of as the most overtly Southern of all the Southern rockers, and there is very little about his conversation, his music, or his general appearance to belie that impression. All, in fact, seem as homegrown and country as in the days when his affiliation with tobacco was considerably more strenuous than it is today—when he picked it for a living in the sunny flatlands of central North Carolina.

He concluded, not surprisingly, that there must be an easier way, and eventually he struck out for Nashville, seeking fortune and maybe a little bit of fame as a sessions musician in the city's armada of recording studios. He hit town in 1967, and played on some memorable albums (Dylan's *Nashville Skyline*, among others), but he never quite made it as a part of the Music Row in-crowd. Almost by default, he decided instead to become a star.

It took a few years, and some experimentation with sounds, for the Nashville producers were steadfastly intolerant of the decibels and rough edges that make his music distinct. So he fled to Macon and cut an album called *Fire On the Mountain*. It sold a million dollars' worth of records, chiefly on the strength of two country-sounding singles that have become, through the sentiments they express, the rallying anthems of the Southern rock movement.

The lesser known of the two, especially outside the South, is a song called "Long Haired Country Boy"—a heartfelt description of a shaggy-headed good ole boy who, like Daniels, has lived through civil rights, Vietnam, rock 'n' roll, marijuana, post-Beatlemania, and all the rest, and has emerged with a curious combination of values and lifestyles. The trappings are different: he smokes grass and lets his hair grow long, while his counterparts of ten or twenty years ago might have been more into duck-tails and beer. But something more basic and Southern is still intact—an attitude, a sort of live-and-let-live affability that is tinged, nevertheless, with defiance.

The song, which is put to the straight country beat of Dickie Betts's dobro, goes like this:

> **People say I'm no good and crazy as a loon,**
> **'Cause I get stoned in the morning,**
> **I get drunk in the afternoon.**
> **Kinda like my old blue-tick hound,**
> **I like to lay around in the shade.**
> **And I ain't got no money, but I damn sure got it made.**
> **And I ain't askin' nobody for nothin',**

**If I can't get it on my own.**
**If you don't like the way I'm livin',**
**You just leave this long haired country boy alone. ©**

"Yeah, that's kind of my philosophy of life," says Daniels with a tug at his sandy-blond whiskers. "I ain't got no image to protect or none of that bullshit. We don't wear no rhinestone Nudie suits; we don't have to worry about nobody knowing that we drink or smoke dope. I don't give a fuck, you know? The kind of people we appeal to don't give a damn. I ain't worried about the Baptists banning us, because they don't come to see us anyway. We're kind of a hard-livin' bunch of people. I think that reflects in our music. You know, we just . . . we just are what we are."

That I-am-what-I-am-and-if-you-don't-like-it-don't-mess-with-me kind of defensiveness is probably one of the more staple characteristics of the Southern psyche, and has been ever since the days of the Civil War. It can be directed from person to person, or from classes of people to classes of people, or even (as has happened a lot during the last hundred years) from the South as a whole toward the rest of the country.

Too many times, of course, it has gotten tangled up in defense of the wrong sorts of causes—slavery and segregation among them—but it always went deeper than the causes themselves, and it has in fact outlived them. The remorseful, guilt-ridden South that danced through the fantasies of homegrown liberals never really materialized, but what has begun to show itself instead is something considerably more substantial: a growing combination of pride and resentment, nurtured in part by the integrated order of the day that prevails in most of the South. We've been through a lot, people are saying, and have been compelled to change whether we wanted to or not. In retrospect, a lot of Southerners are glad about that, but they can't help noticing that serious problems elsewhere became forgotten, somehow, in the moralizing over theirs; and all of it has left them feeling more Southern, and prouder of it, than they ever had before.

When Charlie Daniels recorded his *Fire on The Mountain* album, he put some of those feelings into a song that became—particularly in the South—the biggest hit he ever had. The verses in "The South's Gonna Do It Again" were essentially a celebration of the vitality of Southern music, but the chorus was more general. It goes like this:

So gather round, gather round children,
Get down. Well, just get down children,
Get loud. Well you can be loud and be proud,
And you can be proud here, be proud to a rebel
Cause the South's gonna do it again. ©

It was that kind of risen South spirit that led many Southern rockers to an ardent support of Jimmy Carter's presidential candidacy. Daniels and the others did several benefit performances each, seeking to raise money for the Carter campaign, and in gratitude Carter invited them to play at his inaugural.

It was a peculiar scene at a Presidential ball—the big-band sounds of Glenn Miller or Tommy Dorsey giving way abruptly to the foot-stomping, whoop-em-up beat of Southern country funk. "I never supported a politician before in my life," said Daniels. "But I was around Carter a little bit, and I said, 'There's an honest man.' He was the first honest politician I ever met."

Reminded, however, that there were people who look askance at Carter because he's from the South—who still associate the place of his birth with some dark and murky characteristic that can't be trusted—Daniels replied with a spit in the direction of his styrofoam cup: "It's time people quit thinking that." Then after a pause: "Damn those sons of bitches. I don't owe 'em nothin'. I'm proud of it. Proud of being from the South."

Charlie's irritation comes and goes, depending on his mood. Catch him at a better time, or when he's not being confronted with all the narrow-minded opinions that have been directed at his region, and he's one of the gentlest and least pretentious people you would ever want to meet. But whatever his frame of mind, his pride in the South and his music remains intact. And that kind of pride is what gives Southern music its evangelical air.

There is a shared sense of place that links musicians and audience before the first note is played. The music is part of the landscape, tangible as Georgia red clay and pervasive as Smoky Mountain mists. There are times (especially in the case of Charlie Daniels, Richard Betts, and the Marshall Tucker Band) when the sound is downright country—a testimonial to the renewed power of tradition among a generation in which you might not expect it.

But even more obviously, the music of Daniels and the others represents the sound of change—the intertwined preoccupations with roots and with experimentation that have dominated the recent history of country music (just as a profound combination of nostalgia and future shock has dominated the lives of those who listen). Some of the musical changes have been highly creative, others strictly commercial. No one knows where the whole thing will lead, chiefly because, if you hang around recording centers such as Nashville for very long at all, you realize that the music is heading in a bunch of weird directions all at one time.

# 11

# BACK TO NASHVILLE:
## Commercialism & Creativity

**Will the circle be unbroken?**
—*A. P. Carter*

It began as a gleam in John McEuen's eye, a cheerfully presumptuous impulse that hit him backstage at an Earl Scruggs concert in 1972. Scruggs and his sons were passing through Denver on a tour of one-night stands, and McEuen, the banjo player in a Colorado folk-rock group called the Nitty Gritty Dirt Band, was on hand to hear him.

Like most other banjo pickers in the country, McEuen had long been in awe of Scruggs, the shy and soft-spoken North Carolinian whose three-finger picking style had revolutionized the instrument. McEuen had no way of knowing, of course, that the admiration was mutual, and he had no idea what to expect when, after a few minutes of chatting, he looked at

It was an historic moment in Nashville when the members of the Nitty Gritty Dirt Band gathered at the Woodland Sound studios to cut an album with the greats of old—Merle Travis, Doc Watson, Brother Oswald, Earl Scruggs and more. (Photo by Douglas Green.)

Three generations of country music meet in a Nashville studio as Randy Scruggs
(on autoharp) lays down a song with Doc Watson and Mama Maybelle Carter.
(Photo courtesy the Country Music Foundation Library.)

Emmylou Harris has become another symbol of musical continuity. Her progressive, country-folk-rock style draws heavily on the rich, interlocking traditions of American music. (Photo courtesy Warner/Reprise Records.)

Scruggs and blurted out with a forced casualness: "Say, would be interested in doing an album with us sometime?"

"He looked at me," McEuen remembered later, grinning through his bushy black beard at the memory of Scruggs's legendary humility, "and said, 'Why Ah'd be proud to.'" And so it was that one of the most memorable albums in the history of country music got off the ground. It wound up with the title *Will the Circle Be Unbroken?*, named for the old Carter Family classic, and by the time it was finished it included performances by Scruggs, the Dirt Band, Mama Maybelle Carter, Merle Travis, Doc Watson, Roy Acuff, and Vassar Clements. In addition, some of the younger Nashville sidemen were thrown in for good measure, and the result was a breathtaking display of acoustical country music.

It had been a genuinely historic moment when the full array of pickers gathered at the Woodland Sound studios in Nashville—an unobtrusive oasis in a part of town that's littered with strip-city filling stations, motels, and fast-food restaurants. In those days there was an enormous gulf between the fans of Roy Acuff and the fans of the Nitty Gritty Dirt Band, and in the end it was bridged by the simple expedient of mutual respect.

Like some of the Southern rockers in Macon, and hard-living Charlie Daniels in Tennessee, John McEuen had a deep and long-standing appreciation of the roots of American music. "Those of us in the band," he recalled later, "just wanted to give the older musicians credit for what they've done. We thought the younger generation of fans owed it to themselves, if nothing else, to get into the older forms of music."

All of that had enormous appeal for Scruggs, who had long been fascinated by the concept of musical crossfertilization. Since taking to the road with his sons several years earlier, he had been experimenting with other sounds, blending his distinctive bluegrass style with everything from Memphis blues to Bob Dylan's brand of urban folk. It was, in a way, the culmination of an itch that had begun back in 1960, when Scruggs had appeared one night with saxophone player King Curtis.

"It was a real privilege for me," Scruggs recalled in his Southern drawl that's as slow as the drip of molasses. "We got to jammin' some before the show, and Curtis was so great, I don't know, I just really enjoyed it. I think it was the first time I really realized that the banjo could go well with other kinds of music."

That realization deepened as the sixties progressed and his sons—Gary, Randy, and Steve—grew older. The younger Scruggses were thoroughly versed in their father's music. There was little of the expected teenage rebellion against it, largely because the family relationships were so close. But the boys were young enough to experiment seriously with rock 'n' roll, and Scruggs was open-minded enough to respect their tastes.

"I remember the boys brought the Byrds—Roger McGuinn and some of them—out to the house one time a few years back," Scruggs recalls, "and they sounded so good. I think being associated with some of the younger musicians, it's helped my picking get better and better. I was gettin' pretty stale after doing straight bluegrass all those years."

Scruggs accepted the task of bringing together other participants in the album venture, including Maybelle Carter and Vassar Clements. In another of his characteristic bursts of bravado, McEuen had recruited Doc Watson, and once things began to take shape McEuen's brother, William, worked through Acuff-Rose Publishing to secure the services of Roy Acuff.

Not everyone was delighted with the idea at first. Acuff wasn't, and he grumbled openly about the beards and long hair and other unorthodoxies of the younger musicians. "You're supposed to know a man by the character of his face," he said at one point. "But if you have got your face all covered up with something, well . . ."

Acuff was still skeptical when he arrived at the studio, but after listening to a playback of Merle Travis and the Nitty Gritty Dirt Band doing "I Am a Pilgrim," he nodded his head and strode briskly to the microphone. John McEuen grinned and murmured to nobody in particular, "Well, I guess we passed the test."

Despite Acuff's misgivings, most of the other performers found the whole undertaking an unmitigated delight. For Doc Watson and Merle Travis, especially, it was a significant occasion. It marked the first time that they had met, despite the fact that they are two of the most respected and influential guitar pickers ever to emerge from the mountains of Appalachia.

"You know," said Doc after the initial hellos, "I named my son for you and Eddy Arnold."

"That's what I heard. I appreciate that," replied Travis with self-conscious humility.

"Well," laughed Watson, "I figured that, uh, a little of that good guitar pickin' might rub off on him."

"Look who's talking," said Travis, and with that they were off on a comparison of each other's favorite songs. Bill McEuen quickly turned on the tapes to record the whole event.

In all, the assembled musicians recorded thirty-seven songs for the album, the excitement building continuously as the time approached to do the title cut. When A. P. Carter wrote the song, back in the days when commercial country music was still in its embryonic stages, it was intended as a simple and heartrending ballad about a child's reaction to the death of his mother. It is still that, but the chorus (which is where the song gets its title) has quickly become something more: an ode or anthem to the cause of musical continuity.

Very few people—and least of all such creative musicians as Doc Watson, Earl Scruggs, and John McEuen—expect the music to remain static. But everybody at the Woodland Sound Studios that day believed it ought to remain rooted, and as an album *Will the Circle Be Unbroken?* throbs with the excitement of that feeling.

It was a high point for Nashville, a living embodiment of the fervor and creativity that can flow from crossfertilization. In the years since the session, the Nitty Gritty Dirt Band, the Earl Scruggs Revue, and many of the other musicians who were there have kept the feeling alive, producing in the process some of the best and most imaginative music that they have ever made.

Unhappily, however, there is also an entirely different result that can come from the mixing of country music with other kinds of influences. And three years after the cutting of *Will the Circle Be Unbroken?*, that other possibility revealed itself clearly at a posh uptown concert a few blocks east of Music Row.

There onstage was Barbi Benton, centerfold emeritus and girlfriend of Hugh Hefner, clad, loosely speaking, in a halter-topped pants suit and belting out a medley of Hank Williams hits. As the strains of "Your Cheatin' Heart" and "I Saw The Light" wafted across the hotel ballroom, a handful of well-rounded bunnies paraded through the crowd for the amusement of a few thousand disc jockeys, musicians, and assorted other lost souls who had wandered in off the streets.

Somewhere out there in the rest of Nashville they were celebrating the fiftieth birthday of the Grand Ole Opry. But that historic event seemed a minor preoccupation at best at the Nashville Sheraton. "Looks like this year's party is going to be even better than the last," intoned Hefner, looking simultaneously suave and ill at ease as he took the stage in his blue-jean leisure suit. "We hope you enjoy yourselves."

Hefner had good reason to hope so. He had gone into the country music business a year or so before, and although Playboy Records was doing tolerably well for a new label, most of the artists it had signed were not exactly household names. So Hefner, like any good record executive, had seized upon the presence of a city full of disc jockeys rolling in for their annual convention and willing to celebrate pretty much whatever needed celebrating—from the golden anniversary of a cherished institution to the multiple attributes of Barbi Benton.

He rented himself a hotel, lubricated the scene with free food and whiskey, and paraded out his stable of singers. There was Brenda Pepper, a strapping Alabama lass, wailing out her own version of "When Will I Be Loved" and sounding remarkably unlike Linda Ronstadt. And there was Wynn Stewart, offering up his latest single—a friendly little ballad called "I Think I'm Gonna Kill You and Bury You in a Box About Half Your Size."

For people who were serious about their music, Hefner also brought on Bobby Borchers, a talented songwriter who had written "Jamestown Ferry" for Tanya Tucker; and Mickey Gilley, a charismatic crooner who plays the piano like Jerry Lee Lewis (which is no accident, since the two of them are cousins who grew up together).

But most of all, there was Barbi Benton, wiggling most impressively to the hard-driving beat and insisting with a straight face that Hank Williams had become her idol. There was something implausibly tacky about that particular assertion in that particular setting, but who knows? Music makes strange bedfellows, and vice versa, and the sign on the wall had given fair warning:

"This," it said, "is Playboy Country."

Which was another way of saying that times have changed a lot in the home of the Grand Ole Opry. The music and milieu have taken on an uptown slickness that was never there before, and the fear is growing that the substance will soon be destroyed.

Those fears reached almost hysterical proportions in 1974 when Olivia Newton-John was named country music's Female Vocalist of the Year. Nobody would come right out and publicly assert that she didn't deserve it. She had, after all, had several enormous and identifiably country hits, including "Let Me Be There" and "If You Love Me Let Me Know." But there was a kind of saccharine and unfunky sweetness about her style and arrangements, and there was also her background—that of a good-looking Australian girl who knew so little about the legacy of country music that twenty years after Hank Williams's death, she expressed an interest in meeting him.

Roy Acuff, who was presenting the award, couldn't even bring himself to pronounce her name correctly (it came out something like "Oliver"). And within a few days, a group of stars and semistars whose straight-country credentials were thoroughly in order formed an organization to preserve the purity. Inevitably, of course, there were sour grapes involved. Many of the people who supported the Association of Country Entertainers, as the new group was called, had had conspicuously less success in recent years than Olivia Newton-John.

But there was more to the group than that. It had the backing of some of Nashville's most thoughtful and successful musicians as well—people like Bill Anderson and Dolly Parton—and they were saying things that thousands of country music fans had been saying for years: Keep it country; don't let it be ruined by success; don't lose touch with your fans.

Dolly Parton believes the whole undertaking was worth it in a way. It did at least raise the issue, forcing people to take note of the fact, as Chet Atkins put it, that "music dies when it becomes a parody of itself." But in an absolute sense the goals of ACE were unattainable and unenforceable, entangling themselves in a knot of conflicting conclusions.

What do you say, for example, about Linda Ronstadt and Emmylou Harris, both of whom are generally regarded as pop singers who do a lot of country music? That question, more than any other, was Dolly Parton's imponderable, for although she was interested in limiting the diluting effects of outside influences, she also realized that Emmylou and Linda sing country songs about as well as anyone around.*

She had, in fact, become friends with both of them, discovering that they all had far more in common than she had expected. For starters, they were all the same age (thirty in 1977), and they all grew up with a deep and abiding appreciation of country music. But there were differences as well. While Dolly had grown up in Sevierville, Tennessee, in the final years of intensive Appalachian isolation, Emmylou and Linda had been raised in more sophisticated circumstances (in Birmingham, Alabama, and Tucson, Arizona, respectively), and their musical tastes had been affected by a bombardment of other influences.

Linda Ronstadt believes that diversity of influence has become a universal American experience, and the result, she says, is that the blending of country music with other forms of expression is an absolutely inevitable and irreversible result.

"There isn't any country left," she explained over the sound of her band tuning up before a recent show. "When they closed the Grand Ole Opry, and I know they didn't really close it, but when they moved it out to an amusement park, that sort of officially closed an era. We're all suburban. We all have TVs and radios, and we're all exposed to a lot of different sounds.

"But there's a great thing about this weird hodgepodge of music today," she continued. "People don't have to be so hung up on labels. I'm a pop singer, I guess, but I grew up with country music. I sing it, and it influences most of what I sing, but it isn't the only influence. Music, to me, is music, and it's either good or bad and you judge it on that basis."

Good and bad, of course, are pretty amorphous standards, lying primarily in the tastes of the beholder. But the examples of Linda Ronstadt and Emmylou Harris suggest that there may be a little bit more to the issue.

*Dolly herself began some pretty heavy courting of the rock 'n' roll audience in 1977 with a new album featuring, among other things, a hard-rocking rendition of the old Jackie Wilson hit "Higher and Higher." The people at RCA Records were adamantly convinced—and not without reason—that Dolly could tap into the youthful followings of Ronstadt and Emmylou Harris.

For there is a crucial difference, it seems, between the two of them on the one hand and Olivia Newton-John (and certainly Barbi Benton) on the other.

The difference is that Ronstadt and Harris are remarkably thoughtful and conscientious musicians who have made it a point to understand the heritage of American music—especially country music—and tap into its ongoing vitality. Emmylou, especially, has immersed herself in the Nashville music scene, becoming almost reverential in the presence of such veteran performers as Porter Waggoner, Dolly Parton, and George Jones. She has come to understand the soulful tradition on which they draw, and the understanding shows.

To appreciate the effect of such a deep-seated musical identity, you need only to spend a few hours at an Emmylou Harris concert and revel in the magnificently expressive qualities of her shimmering-vibrato voice. At times she sounds like the quintessential female shit-kicker as she moves through songs like Merle Haggard's "Tonight the Bottle Let Me Down" or Wayne Kemp's "Feelin' Single—Seein' Double."

"It's just an old drinkin' song," she says in introducing the latter number, which tells the story of a mischievous married girl who gets drunk, engages in some unintended amorous pursuits, and emerges with no regrets at all.

Emmylou grins when the song is over, and says in a soft, shy voice, "It don't mean nothin'."

Plenty of her songs do mean something, however. She is at her best when she's doing sad and easy love songs about believable relationships—Susanna Clark's "I'll Be Your San Antone Rose," Paul McCartney's "Here, There and Everywhere," or her own "Boulder to Birmingham," which she wrote with some polishing help from Bill Danoff. Her voice, in those situations, alternates between a belting sort of power and a fragile, throbbing clarity that is all her own.

There just isn't anybody, in fact, who sings country songs with any better feel or any more feeling; and it's not even a matter of talent—at least not entirely. Olivia Newton-John, for example, is a competent performer, who has gotten a much bummer rap than she deserves from the reviewers of country music. She does no real violence to the country tradition. But she can't pour out the emotion of Ronstadt or Harris, because she simply doesn't have the *feel*—the instinctive, deep-down grasping of where the music has been.

Barbi Benton takes the problem a step further. She not only lacks the feel and the background, but she is also remarkably devoid of talent. She owes her career almost entirely to the monied status of her boyfriend and to today's high-powered production techniques, which can make the featured performer, if necessary, a less integral part of the recorded result.

That is a crucial change for country music. There was a time when, if you were bad, you sounded bad and there was no way around it. It is ironic that one of the people most responsible for changing that hard and cold reality, and opening the floodgates of modern mediocrity, is one of the most talented musicians ever to come through Nashville—a guitar-picking expatriate from the southern Appalachians by the name of Chet Atkins.

Atkins became the man in charge at RCA's first Nashville recording studio in the midfifties, and quickly began raising eyebrows and setting trends with his pop-oriented productions of such country stars as Jim Reeves and Don Gibson. Blending influences was something that came natural to him, for his whole career as a guitar picker had been one uninterrupted burst of mongrelization and nonconformity.

He was and is, to be sure, a country guitarist—simply because he has in fact been a country boy, a shy and malnourished mountain kid, raised amid grinding poverty in the whistle-stop town of Luttrell, Tennessee.

During his boyhood days most of the mountain musicians played guitar with a pick. But early on, Atkins chose to pluck the instrument with his fingers—initially because of the influence of his stepfather, who didn't know any better. Later, he heard Merle Travis finger-picking on the radio, and made a conscious decision that he, Chet Atkins, would play the guitar that way from that day forth.

Atkins was restless with any one influence, however, and drew his early musical inspiration from all kinds of other sources, in addition to Travis, including Jimmie Rodgers, Blind Lemon Jefferson, Benny Goodman, and the other pop artists he could hear on the radio. In the forties, after he had turned professional, Atkins also became caught up in classical guitar—fascinated by Segovia and a musician's musician from France named Django Reinhardt. Meanwhile he kept in determined touch with country music, at one point playing rhythm guitar for the Carter Family, and later doing backup work for the likes of Hank Williams.

Because of such a background, it was predictable that he would experiment a little when RCA picked him as their man in Nashville. Some of the experimentation came on the rockabilly sessions with Elvis, and later the Everly Brothers, but it also spilled over into acts considered more country. He put a bass drum on Don Gibson's "I Can't Stop Loving You" and "Oh Lonesome Me," and slicked up the production considerably nearly every time he went into the studio with Jim Reeves.

In Reeves, Atkins knew he had the kind of polished and mellow entertainer who could cross over into the pop market, and so he intentionally made some compromises in the purity of the product, using symphonic-sounding violins and leaving out the more earthy and backwoodsy sounds of fiddles and steel guitars.

"We were consciously trying for pop sales and . . . at that time you couldn't get a record played pop if it had steel on it," Atkins told *Rolling Stone*'s Chet Flippo in a lengthy interview in 1976. "That only happened a few years ago when Dylan came in with steel. But I always tried, like with Reeves, I tried to make good records that had a pretty sound."

Generally, he succeeded. But he also opened the door to other possibilities, and the ultimate result was the uptown Nashville Sound—the big, almost Las Vegas-y productions laden with orchestral strings and backup voices that sound about as country as the Mormon Tabernacle Choir. And for that, Chet has apologized.

"Of course I had a lot to do with changing country [music]," said Atkins in an interview with *People* magazine, "and I apologize. We did it to broaden the appeal and to keep making records different, to surprise the public.

"I hate to see country music going uptown," he continued, "because it's the wrong uptown. We're about to lose our identity and get all mixed up with other music. We were always a little half-assed anyway, but a music dies when it becomes a parody of itself."

No doubt the apology was straight from the heart, but Atkins is also intelligent enough to know that there were forces far larger than himself behind the slickness and commercialism that have become some of the key characteristics of modern-day Nashville. Commercialism feeds on itself, and when the city's music industry began pulling in more and more profits in the fifties and sixties, the business interests downtown became slowly and dimly aware of an eye-opening truth: They were sitting—all too passively, they soon concluded—on an untapped vein of prime vinyl gold.

Tourism, the city fathers realized, was a largely underutilized resource, and for obvious economic reasons that's a situation nearly any place wants to correct. If you don't mind your streets being littered with camera-clicking outsiders, the tourist trade represents a remarkably enticing opportunity to pad your city's coffers with somebody else's money.

It wasn't that Nashville didn't have any tourists. For years the Packards and pickup trucks had rumbled in from the hill country and battled for parking space near the Ryman Auditorium. But all of that was simply a quaint and rustic prologue to the interlocking Jet Age visions of the Chamber of Commerce, the policymakers at radio station WSM, and a spin-off booster group known as the Nashville Plus Steering Committee.

The Chamber of Commerce had long been interested in a downtown Hyatt-Regency-type convention hotel. WSM was hatching plans to replace the dilapidating Ryman with something more spectacular, and the Nashville Plus Committee had begun to envision a face-lifting of Music Row, centering on a four-lane thoroughfare to channel the curiosity seekers through what had always been a fairly nondescript area. Since the membership of all three groups was inclined to overlap, the compatibility of the projects soon became apparent; and following a determined and high-powered push, their goals (and plenty more besides) have become a reality. The tourists are flocking in like sheep, and they are not the only ones who are impressed by what they see.

"Man," said a young songwriter named Vince Matthews, as he strolled along Music Row a few months back, "all us hillbillies have come uptown, you know? Or maybe I should say that uptown has come to us."

But as Matthews well knows, there are some problems there for people who are engaged in his line of work and who are serious about their craft. The commercializing forces can be a little devastating when they are really unleashed, for the common denominator of slickness—whether of the music or the landscape—is an overriding concern for what the masses will want. The concern is inevitable for a business executive, but it can be hard on the dreams of the hungry young picker-poets who wander into town with their guitar cases strapped to their backs and a handful of songs wadded away in their jeans.

Geoff Morgan has been luckier than most. He is an example of a young man learning to cope. But the tension that he faces, like a lot of those who made it before him, is that it's entirely possible to cope too well—to adjust too completely to Nashville's commercial expectations.

Morgan arrived in the city in 1973—a young, redheaded Connecticut Yankee with a winning smile and loads of talent. He settled in and then began the timid and uncertain process of knocking on doors and pushing his songs, including one called "Son of the Father," which may be the definitive composition about a near-miss family relationship. It goes like this:

> **With a smile painted on his face**
> **His daddy spent his life knocking on the door**
> **Born of strange and restless soul**
> **He always seems to miss what he was looking for**
> **And now his eyes are growing old**
> **Eyes that never found the gold**
> **And the son of the father lives alone.**
>
> **He came home from the war**
> **He'd done all right, he could learn the hating**
> **The boat landed on the shore**
> **He did what was right, he married who was waiting**
> **But now their love is growing old**
> **A love that never found the gold**
> **And the son of the father lives alone.**
>
> **They raised an only son**
> **And like the folks next door, they called it a family**
> **But he became a lonely one**
> **They tried to give him more, but he grew only angry**
> **And now the boy is growing old**
> **The boy who never found the gold**
> **And the son of the father lives alone.** ©

The melody is sad and moving, and with Morgan's country-clear, Willie-

Nelsonish kind of voice, it's an honest-to-God tearjerker in the best sense of the term. The only trouble was that because the subject matter was not very commercial nobody showed much interest in recording it—or any of Morgan's other stuff for that matter—until he signed a writing contract with Pi-Gem Publishing.

Pi-Gem is run by Tom Collins, who is best known these days as the producer who helped make Ronnie Milsap a superstar. Collins is a pro. He knows what will sell, and has sought to generate the same instinct in Morgan. He may well have succeeded, for within a short time after their association began, Morgan wrote a hit for Dickie Lee—a washed-up rock singer who is trying to salvage a career on the country market. The record, called "Busiest Memory In Town," became by far the biggest seller that Lee had had since his star began its current ascent.

The other thing worth nothing about the song, however, is that it's not really that good. It's not bad; it's just not the kind of thing that a person with Geoff Morgan's ability ought to be very proud of, and in fact he's not. But nearly every day he heads for his homemade studio around nine in the morning and quits each afternoon about five—writing an average of two songs a day, many of which are about as noteworthy as "Busiest Memory."

It's not that Morgan has sold out. He is a sharp fellow with few illusions, and he has come to see success in the music business as a matter of hard work as well as native talent. He is willing to pay his dues, he says, and work for the day when he is established enough to do what he wants. Morgan may have the talent to pull it off, but some of his more artistic songwriting compatriots (Guy Clark, Steve Earl, and Robin and Linda Williams, among others) are worried about him. They are convinced that in poetic, if not commercial, terms, he's playing with fire. They say that his have the ring of famous last words, and in his case especially, they are afraid of a waste.

My own view is that Morgan will be okay. He is one of the more impressive singers and writers to come along in a while, and he ought to be able to survive a temporary flirtation with formula. But whatever happens to Geoff, there are other people around Nashville whose careers are an implicit affirmation of the power of the country tradition. They are people like Vince Matthews—fire-in-the-belly songwriters who are tempted and buffeted by the lures of commercial success, but who cling with instinctive (and maybe even unintentional) tenacity to their own brand of artistic integrity. They may be crazy, often are; but as Johnny Cash once said of Vince, they write what they live and live what they write. And in an odd and fragile way, they are the modern-day hope of country music.

# 12

# VINCE

**That great speckled bird sang her song in his ear**
**Whisperin' words of magic that only Vince could hear.***

*—Larry Wilkerson and Shel Silverstein*

It was a rainy Nashville night, the dregs of winter, as Vince Matthews and his Budweiser stumbled down a back-alley stairway and ducked into the automobile of a friend. Vince was entering that happy stage of inebriation in which his tongue is unleashed on a variety of philosophical rampages, ranging from the evils of Richard Nixon to the trials and tribulations of writing country songs.

The latter subject is actually most interesting to him, for, like most people, Vince finds himself one of the world's more fascinating topics of conversation. Unlike most people, he is probably right.

He has been knocking around Nashville for a dozen years, writing songs that run the gamut from terrible to poignant, and building (sometimes consciously) a richly deserved reputation as the quintessential crazy, mixed-up, manic depressive, unlucky, when-you're-hot-you're-hot, when-you're-not-you're-not kind of songwriter who is still hanging in there and no doubt will be as long as he's breathing.

"You gotta live it, man," he said with slurry-tongued sincerity as the car bounced gingerly along the alleyway potholes. And with that he launched into the story of how he once hitchhiked to Chicago with five dollars in his pocket, arrived with only one, and passed three days in a drainage culvert wondering how to spend a lonesome dollar bill.

Eventually he said to hell with it, and threw it away. After miraculously failing to starve, he somehow wound up in Nashville again, where he wrote a song about the whole experience. Johnny Cash heard it, recorded it, and before long "Wrinkled, Crinkled, Wadded Dollar Bill" had made it to the top of the country music charts, and Vince became temporarily rich.

"I think," he said, as his mind wandered reluctantly back to the present, "that it's called casting your bread on the water. At least that's what Jesus called it."

The parallels between Jesus and Vince are not overwhelming, however. He has a lot of traits that Jesus no doubt would have admired, but throwing away the dollar was more an offering to art than to religion, and in an odd sort of way it typified Matthews's whole career. There is nothing he loves more than a wallet full of money, but he has steadfastly refused to become a slave to its pursuit. And the refusal has kept him pure—a personification of the uncommercialized side of country music.

Matthews was born in the west Tennessee town of Waverly on May 3, 1942, and spent his teenage years listening to the rockabilly outpourings of Sun Records in Memphis and trying his hand at some amateur songwriting. Some time around his twentieth birthday he headed east to Nashville, and he cut a pretty impressive figure when he hit town—a bright and energetic young man, with the high Cherokee cheekbones and the jet-black hair of a forgotten Tennessee ancestor.

He had little trouble landing a job in an advertising firm, then later in the office of a commercial artist. But a friend named Bill Brook (who had written a song for Chubby Checker) showed him how to approximate the

A, F, and D chords on a guitar, and on the same afternoon Vince sat down and wrote twenty-eight songs. They were terrible. He was hooked, however, and kept on dabbling until finally, in the late winter of 1963, he helped compose a maudlin ballad called "Hobo and a Rose."

"Don Vincent and I wrote it on a Sunday," Vince recalled. "We pitched it to Webb Pierce on Monday, and he cut it on Wednesday. I thought, 'Jeez, this is the easiest thing I ever did. I think I'll do it every day.' I've been hitting off and on ever since—mostly off, I might add."

The gyrations between high-riding success and abject, starvation-level failure have defined Vince's career, and the capricious pummeling has taken its toll on his ego and all-around psychological functioning. His songs kept getting better and better, but his ratio of success remained frustratingly constant. There were some definite high points: He wrote "Bob" for the Willis Brothers, which was one of the most serious records that they ever did, and along with Jim Casey he wrote a song called "Toast of '45" for Sammi Smith. It told the story of an over-the-hill movie actress, and established Matthews as a writer with a deep-seated understanding of the human condition.

It established him, that is, among the other artist-types around Nashville—but not among the record-buying public. For the dry spells continued to plague him, and the eye-opening fact of the matter was that they had little relationship to anything—to how hard he was working, or how well he was writing, or how deeply he wanted to succeed.

That kind of psychological environment will leave you with a finely honed sense of the absurd, and it may have been for that very reason that Vince fell in so compatibly with Kris Kristofferson. Kristofferson arrived in town several years after Vince had already established a toehold, and like Matthews he found himself bouncing around between his own basic confidence in what he could do and the hard and cold fact that no one was listening. So the two of them took what comfort they could in a loose confederation of other Young Turks, a sort of artistic cabal consisting of Mickey Newbury, Townes Van Zandt, Billy Swann, and a few dozen more—sharing songs, joints, and good times, and boosting one another's creative instincts.

Vince was (and still is) genuinely stunned by Kristofferson's ability with words, and during the lean years when the Music Row decision-makers weren't paying much attention, Kris would bring over his latest compositions and lay his ego on the line for a Matthews critique. Sometimes he listened to what Vince had to say, and other times, fortunately, he didn't. Once, for example, Kristofferson brought over a brand-new ballad called "Me and Bobby McGee," and Vince told him it was great except for the line about freedom being just another word for nothing left to lose.

"Doesn't fit," Vince insisted. "Disrupts the story line."

Matthews will tell the story on himself with considerable delight these days—laughing in his semimaniacal way about how Kristofferson's words have become a sure bet for any updated versions of *Bartlett's Familiar Quotations*. Then, with another slurp at his Budweiser, he will turn suddenly serious and affirm with a sheepish nod of his head that "there was actually a time when I thought I was as smart as ole Kris."

It's a revealing confession, an unintended testimonial to the fact that his friendship with Kristofferson has been a double-edged reality. On the one hand it has certainly helped him, for Kristofferson has pushed his songs, plugged him on national TV, and even, on occasion, shoved him onstage for concert appearances. But on the other hand Kris became famous and Vince never did, and that's a tough one to take no matter how well you and your ego get along. In Matthews's case, the relationship with his self-esteem has always been a little bit turbulent, and he has spent more hours than he cares to remember wondering why he wasn't born a genius.

Actually, however, that may be the wrong question, for at his best Vince can write songs with anybody. Johnny Cash once maintained that a Matthews composition called "Melva's Wine" was the "best contemporary folk song in American music." And "On Susan's Floor"—recorded in equally moving versions by Gordon Lightfoot and Hank Williams, Jr.—has its own minicult following among country musicians.

So the barrier between Vince and stardom is not really his brain. But it is something equally basic: it's his voice. He can't sing a lick. Some people would argue, of course, that Kristofferson can't either, but Vince is to Kristofferson as Kristofferson is to Mario Lanza; and to understand the full weight of that reality, you had only to accompany Vince one night a few years back to an Exit Inn appearance by Mickey Newbury.

Newbury is one of the more magnificent vocalists on the country scene, with a voice that is mellow and strong and throbbing with emotion. When he turns it loose on his own compositions—songs like "Heaven Help the Child" and "An American Trilogy"—jaws will drop in the crowd, eyes will become riveted to the front of the room, and all other sounds will dry up with the kind of awe and deference that the occasion demands.

At least that's what usually happens. But if Vince is along you never quite know what to expect, and on this particular night he was so far on his way toward chemical alteration that he simply couldn't contain himself. He began to sing along from his back-row seat, softly at first, but soon with all the power and sincerity of a wounded dog or a cow in labor.

Through it all, he retained a sort of boozy and beatific tolerance toward the stares of hatred and disbelief that were being cast in his direction. However, when a waiter began taking whispered orders for drinks during one particularly moving number, Vince lurched up to him and demanded that he please show respect for an artist of Mickey Newbury's caliber.

But that, as people around Nashville are fond of saying, is just Vince. He has a fierce and unshakable loyalty toward people he respects, and the feeling is very often mutual. When he decided a few years back, for example, that he wanted to cut an album, Kris Kristofferson and Shel Silverstein agreed to produce it, and Johnny Cash wrote some liner notes and even whistled background on one of the cuts. And surprisingly enough, given Vince's limitations in front of a microphone, most people who heard it thought it was a pretty good record, especially in its content. It was a concept album titled *Kingston Springs Suite* and telling the story of Kingston Springs, Tennessee, a tiny, hill-country town that you could plunk down with equal validity almost anywhere in middle America.

Matthews lived in Kingston Springs for seven years, developing a strong affection for its people, and he brought that feeling alive with songs about an old man dying, a young girl leaving town (because she believed, erroneously, that no one cared about her), and a village blacksmith who was also a dispenser of down-home wisdom.

Counting the time he spent writing the songs, Vince worked on the album off and on for more than five years. He couldn't find a record label to back the project, but it developed into an obsession with him and he went into the studio anyway. He says he spent fifty thousand dollars of his own money (actually money that he didn't really have yet) buying studio time, paying musicians, and even having half a dozen records pressed in order to try to sell the finished product to a major label.

But even with the intercession of his well-connected friends, nobody was interested, and Vince found himself financially and spiritually in considerable debt—especially since he wasn't getting any songs cut by other artists. The year 1974 came and went before he had earned a penny, and the prospects didn't appear too much better in the early months of 1975. So Vince said good-bye to Kingston Springs and Nashville and headed for New York, hoping desperately that greener pastures might be waiting somehow amid the concrete canyons. They weren't.

But then, in one of those unexplainable quirks that have characterized Vince's flirtations with country music, a pair of newcomers named Gene Watson and Crystal Gayle decided to record some songs that he had written several years earlier. Watson's version of "Love in the Hot Afternoon" went to the top of the charts, and Miss Gayle (who is Loretta Lynn's little sister) did almost as well with "This Is My Year for Mexico"— the story of a housewife trapped by habit and dreaming of the places she would go if her spirit were only a little bit freer.

Charley Pride soon cut a masculine version of Crystal Gayle's hit; Hank Williams, Jr., went into the studio with "On Susan's Floor," and suddenly—thirteen years after he'd first breezed into Nashville— Vince Matthews was hot commercial property. He signed a writing contract with Peer-Southern, a prestigious company headed by Ralph Peer, Jr., whose father, Ralph Sr., of Okeh Records, had wandered down from New York in the twenties to record such ambitious hillbillies as Pop Stoneman, Jimmie Rodgers, and the Carter Family.

One of the first songs Vince wrote after his deal with Peer was titled "Who Was Bradley Kincaid?"—an ode of sorts to the college-educated Kentucky guitarist who had headed north in the early twenties to become a star on the WLS Barn Dance. All of that was symbolic to Vince, for he is, among other things, a student of the country tradition, and captivated by the concept that his own niche is being carved, somehow, by an inscrutable destiny—carrying with it the inevitable does of artistic suffering.

All of that may be simple presumption or conceit, but then again it may not. For Vince has lived and embodied all the things that give country music its power: He has known the sting of failure and the whiffs of occasional prosperity. He has been drunk, lonesome, lovesick, and hungry, and through it all he has clung to the basic sensitivity and human compassion that have always been the cornerstone of good country music.

"I like Vince a lot," says Johnny Cash with a nod of somber finality. "He's probably one of the greatest writers this business has ever had. I sure would like to see him make it."

Personally, I don't think it will make a whole lot of difference to Vince, for he is equally at home cruising around Nashville in a Cadillac he can't afford, or selling the damn thing and hitching a ride with a friend. Which is what he did a little while back, and as we rumbled down the alleyway toward a sleazy little tavern where the pickers gather for pinball and beer, he began to talk about the deal he had struck with Peer—a songwriter's dream, he affirmed with a sweeping gesture that sent the rearview mirror spinning into nonalignment.

"Oops, sorry," he said, making a feeble attempt at repairing the damage. "Anyway, man, I ain't saying it's been easy, but hell, I'm only thirty-three. That's not too bad, is it? I got two songs on the charts, I got a good deal with a publisher, hell I just might make it this time. But then," he said, opening the door and pausing half in and half out for an eloquent summation, "I s'pose I've said that before..."

As he grinned and went trudging off into the Nashville rain, humming off-key and wobbling toward the fog-shrouded honky-tonk, you had the feeling, somehow, that country music just might survive its current bout with success.

# APPENDIX

### The Lyrics of Country Music

No matter how much you analyze country music, it's hard to improve on the eloquence of the people who produce it. The songs that follow tell their own stories, and the purpose of this appendix is to afford them that chance.

They are, I think, fifty-five of the best and most representative songs ever written. Certainly they were among those foremost in my mind as I wrote this book. Many are quoted in part, or at least alluded to, in the text. Several are not, but only because I couldn't work them in without disrupting the flow of my own ideas.

Most of these songs were hits, or were included in heavy-selling or influential albums. But here again, there are deliberate exceptions. There are no doubt dozens of singers and songwriters around Nashville who have never heard of Sarah Ogan Gunning or her music. But within its own sphere that music was extremely important, and her songs have become solidly embedded in the legacy I've tried to describe.

To be sure, some arbitrary factors affected my selections. One is the matter of my own personal tastes. Another is the willingness of publishing companies to allow their songs to be included. There are no Kris Kristofferson compositions, for example, simply because his publisher refused permission to print them.

But those songs that are included—the hits and the non-hits together—do give an excellent feel for the diverse and evolving sensibilities of country music.

F. G.

## Old Dogs, Children and Watermelon Wine

How old do you think I am? he said.
I said well I didn't know.
He said, I turned 65 about eleven months ago.

I was sittin' in Miami pouring blended whiskey down
When this old grey black gentleman was cleaning up the lounge.
There wasn't anyone around 'cept this old man and me
The guy who ran the bar was watching Ironsides on TV.
Uninvited, he sat down and opened up his mind
On old dogs and children and watermelon wine.

Ever had a drink of watermelon wine? he asked.
He told me all about it, though I didn't answer back.
Ain't but three things in this world that's worth a solitary dime
But old dogs and children and watermelon wine.

He said, women think about theyselves when menfolk ain't around
And friends are hard to find when they discover that you're down.
He said, I tried it all when I was young and in my natural prime
Now it's old dogs and children and watermelon wine.

Old dogs care about you even when you mistakes
And God bless little children while they're still too young to hate.
When he moved away I found my pen and copied down that line
'Bout old dogs and children and watermelon wine.

I had to catch a plane up to Atlanta that next day.
As I left for my room I saw him picking up my change.
That night I dreamed in peaceful sleep of shady summertime
Of old dogs and children and watermelon wine.

*By Tom T. Hall © 1972 Hallnote Music.*
*Used by permission. All rights reserved.*

## This Stranger (My Little Girl)

Today for her it's only been
Thirteen years of livin'
And for me it's been a wonderful 13 years of givin'.
She grows taller every day
And farther from my world.
God help me reach this stranger
My little girl.

Music I can't understand
Replaced her nursery rhymes.
No longer can I even guess
What's running through her mind.
Her long straight hair has forgotten
Ribbons and soft curls.
God please protect this stranger
My little girl.

Can she hear the worried sound
In her Mom's conversation?
Can she see the anguish in my look of desperation?
Can she feel my love for her
Pulling against her world?
I love her so, this stranger
My little girl.

Has she so soon forgotten
Just how close we used to be
And how when something troubled her
She'd always run to me?
But Mom can't solve her problems
She keeps locked inside her world.
God help me reach this stranger
My little girl.

Can she hear the worried sound
In her Mom's conversation?
Can she see the anguish in my look of desperation?
Can she feel my love for her
Pulling against her world?
I love her so, this stranger
My little girl.

## Let Him Roll

He was a wino tried and true
Done about everything there is to do
He'd worked on freighters and he'd worked in bars
He'd worked on farms and he'd worked on cars

It was white port put that look in his eyes
That grown men get when they need to cry
We sat down on the curb to rest
And his head just fell down on his chest

He says "Every single day it gets
Just a little bit harder to handle and yet..."
Then he lost the thread and his mind got cluttered
And the words just rolled off down the gutter

He was elevator man in a cheap hotel
In exchange for the rent on a one room cell
And he was old in years beyond his time
No thanks to the world and the white port wine

So he say. "Son" he always called me son—
He said "life for you has just begun"
Then he told me the story I'd heard before
How he fell in love with a Dallas whore

He could cut through the years to the very night
That it ended in a whorehouse fight
And she turned his last proposal down
In favor of being a girl about town

Now it's been 17 years right in line
And he ain't been straight none of the time
It's too many years of fightin' the weather
And too many nights of not bein' together

So he died

And when they went through his personal effects
In among the stubs from the welfare checks
Was a crumblin' picture of a girl in a door
An address in Dallas and nothin' more

The welfare people provided the priest
And the couple from the mission down the street
Sang "Amazing Grace" and no one cried
'Cept some lady in black way off to the side

## WATERMELON WINE
**194**

We all left and she's standin' there
Black veil coverin' the silver hair
And old one-eyed John said her name was Alice
She used to be a whore in Dallas

So let him roar, Lord, let him roll
I bet he's gone to Dallas, rest his soul
Let him roll, let him roar
He always said that heaven was just a Dallas whore
Let him roar, Lord, let him roll
I bet he's gone to Dallas, rest his soul

## Where I'm Bound

It's a long and dusty road
And a hot and heavy load
And the people that you meet aren't always kind.
Some are bad and some are good
Some have done the best they could
Some have tried to ease my troubled mind.

I can't help but wonder where I'm bound
Where I'm bound
I can't help but wonder where I'm bound.

I've been around this land
Just adoin' the best I can
Tryin' to find what I was meant to do
And the faces that I see
Are as worried as can be
And I think they're wondering too.

I can't help but wonder where I'm bound
Where I'm bound
I can't help but wonder where I'm bound.

I had a friend back home
Til he started out to roam.
Now I hear he's out by Frisco Bay.
Well sometimes when I've had a few
His voice comes singin' through
And I'm goin' out to see him some old day.

Now if you see me passin' by
And you sit and wonder why
You weren't meant to be a rambler too,
Well nail your shoes to the kitchen floor
And lace em up and bar the door
And thank the Lord for the roof that's over you.

I can't help but wonder where I'm bound
Where I'm bound
I can't help but wonder where I'm bound.

*Arranged and adapted with lyrics added by Clay
Smith. © Clay Music Corp. Used by permission.*

# CHAPTER 1

## When the Wagon Was New

There's an old rusty wagon
That's left to rot away
It's the one the family rode in
Back in the good ole days
People all loved their neighbor
Everybody was so free
And ridin' in the brand new wagon
Was something to see

*Chorus:*
I can see my daddy sitting on the wagon seat
Mom in an old sun bonnet
She looked so nice and neat
Children all in the wagon
Grandma and Grandpa too
Oh we used to go to church on Sunday
When the wagon was new

Red wheels were on the wagon
And the body it was green
But we were all as happy
As ridin' in a limousine
People used to gather round
From o'er the mountain side
Take a look at the brand new wagon
And all take a ride

*Repeat chorus.*

The automobiles are here now
And the wagon days are through
The airplanes are a-hummin'
Good neighbors are so few
Everybody's in a hurry
To get the money to take you through
Well, we didn't need much money
When the wagon was new

## CHAPTER 2

### Cold, Cold Heart

I tried so hard, my dear, to show
That you're my every dream
Yet you're afraid each thing I do
Is just some evil scheme
A memory from your lonesome past
Keeps us so far apart
Why can't I free your doubtful mind
And melt your cold, cold heart?

Another love before my time
Made your heart sad and blue
And so my heart is paying now
For things I didn't do
In anger, unkind words are said
That make the teardrops start
Why can't I free your doubtful mind
And melt your cold, cold heart?

You'll never know how much it hurts
To see you sit and cry
You know you need and want my love
Yet you're afraid to try

Why do you run and hide from life
To try, it just ain't smart
Why can't I free your doubtful mind
And melt your cold, cold heart?

There was a time when I believed
That you belonged to me
But now I know your heart is shackled
To a memory
The more I learn to care for you
The more we drift apart
Why can't I free your doubtful mind
And melt your cold, cold heart?

## I'm So Lonesome I Could Cry

Hear that lonesome whippoorwill?
He sounds too blue to fly
The midnight train is whining low
I'm so lonesome I could cry.

I've never seen a night so long
When time goes crawling by
The moon just went behind a cloud
To hide its face and cry.

Did you ever see a robin weep
When leaves begin to die?
That means he's lost the will to live
I'm so lonesome I could cry.

The silence of a falling star
Lights up a purple sky
And as I wonder where you are
I'm so lonesome I could cry.

## Are You Sure Hank Done It This Way

Lord it's the same old tune, fiddle and guitar
Where do we take it from here
Rhinestone suits and new shiny cars
It's been the same way for years
We need a change

Somebody told me when I came to Nashville
Son you finally got it made
Old Hank made it here
We're all sure that you will
But I don't think Hank done it this way
Naw, I don't think Hank done it this way

Ten years on the road making one night stands
Speedin' my young life away
Tell me one more time just so's I'll understand
Are you sure Hank done it this way?
Did ole Hank really do it this way?

Lord I've seen the world with a five piece band
Looking at the back side of me
Singing my songs
One of his now and then
But I don't think Hank done 'em this way
I don't think Hank done 'em this way

## T For Texas (Blue Yodel)

T for Texas, T for Tennessee
T for Texas, T for Tennessee
T for Thelma, that gal that made a wreck out of me.

If you don't want me, Mama, you sure don't have to stall
If you don't want me, Mama, you sure don't have to stall
'Cause I can get more women than a passenger train can haul.

I'm gonna buy me a pistol just as long as I'm tall
I'm gonna buy me a pistol just as long as I'm tall

I'm gonna shoot poor Thelma just to see her jump and fall.

I'm going where the water drinks like cherry wine
I'm going where the water drinks like cherry wine
'Cause the Georgia water tastes like turpentine.

I'm gonna buy me a shotgun with a great long shiny barrel
I'm gonna buy me a shotgun with a great long shiny barrel
I'm gonna shoot that rounder that stole away my gal.

Rather drink muddy water and sleep in a hollow log
Rather drink muddy water and sleep in a hollow log
Than to be in Atlanta, treated like a dirty dog.

*By Jimmie Rodgers. © Copyright 1928*
*by Peer International Corporation Copyright renewed. Used by permission.*

## CHAPTER 3

### Down on the Farm

When a boy I used to dwell
In a home I love so well
Far away among the clover and the bees
Where the morning glory vine
'Round our cabin door did twine
And the robin red breast sings among the trees

There were brothers young and gay
And a father old and gray
And a mother dear to keep me from all harm
There I spent life's happy hours
Running wild among the flowers
In my boyhood happy home, down on the farm

But today as I draw near
To the home I love so dear
A stranger comes to meet me at the door
Around the place there's many a change
And the faces all seem strange
Not a loved one comes to greet me as of yore

And my mother dear is laid
Neath the elm tree's white shade
Where the golden summer sun shines bright and warm

And near the old fireplace
I see a stranger's face
In my father's old armchair, down on the farm

*Traditional (as sung by Asa Martin and Doc Roberts)*
*Gennett Records, 1930*


## Clay County Miner

He's a poor man 'cause mining's all he's known
And miners don't get rich loading coal
He's a sick man 'cause that coal dust took its stand
But he don't expect to get no help from that operator man.

*Chorus:*
Well it's good-bye Old Timer, I guess our time has come
Those water holes, that dirty coal dust eating up our lungs
We'll leave this world just as poor as the day we saw the sun
Well it's good-bye Old Timer, all our mining is done.

I remember the time when I could load more coal than any man
Now my health is gone, buried down in that dirty ground
And they've taken away my rights, privilege to be a man
But I know I can't tell all that to the operator man.

*Repeat chrous.*

Remember Old Timer, when we were little kids
When we'd talk about our mining days when we'd get grown and big
But now we're old, broken men, they don't need us around
Though we gave our lives to make them rich, they won't give us a dime.

*Repeat chorus.*

*By Hazel Dickens. © Happy Valley Music*
*Used by permission.*


## The Coming of the Roads

Oh now that our mountain is growing
With people hungry for wealth
How come it's you that's a-going
And I'm left alone by myself?

We used to hunt the cool caverns
Deep in our forest of green
Then came the roads and the taverns
And you found a new love, it seems.

Once I had you and the wild wood
Now it's just dusty roads
And I can't help from blaming
Your going
On the coming
The coming of the roads.

Look how they've cut all to pieces
Our ancient poplar and oak
And the hillsides are stained with the greases
That burn up the heavens with smoke.

We used to curse the bold crewmen
Who stripped our earth of its ore
Now you've changed and you've gone over to them
And you've learned to love what you hated before.

Once I thanked God for my treasure
Now, like rust, it corrodes
And I can't help from blaming
Your going
On the coming
The coming of the roads.

*Words and Music: Billy Edd Wheeler. © Copyright 1964, 1971*
*by Quartet Music, Inc., and Bexhill Music Corp.*
*Used by permission.*

## They Can't Put It Back

Down in the valley 'bout a mile from me
Where the crows no longer fly,
There's a great big earth-movin' monster-machine
Stands ten stories high.
The ground he can eat, it's a sight;
He can rip out a hundred tons at a bite.
He can eat up the grass, it's a fact,
But he can't put it back!

## WATERMELON WINE
### 202

They come and tell me I've got to move,
Make way for that big machine;
But I ain't a-movin' unless they kill me,
Like they killed the fish in my stream.
But look at that big machine go;
Took that shady grove a long time to grow.
He can rip it out with one whack,
But he can't put it back.

I never was one to walk in lines,
Picket with placards, or carry signs.
But maybe I'm behind the times.

*Words and music by Billy Edd Wheeler. © 1966, 1971
by Quartet Music, Inc., and Bexhill Music Corp.
Used by permission.*


## Dreadful Memories

Dreadful memories, how they linger
How they ever flood my soul,
How the workers and their children
Died from hunger and from cold.

Hungry fathers, wearied mothers
Living in those dreadful shacks,
Little children cold and hungry
With no clothing on their backs.

Dreadful gun-thugs and stool-pigeons
Always flock around our door.
What's the crime that we've committed?
Nothing, only that we're poor.

Oh, those memories, how they haunt me
Makes me want to organize
Makes me want to help the workers
Make them open up their eyes.

When I think of all the heartaches
And all the things that we've been through,
Then I wonder how much longer
And what a working man can do.

Really, friends, it doesn't matter
Whether you are black or white.
The only way you'll ever change things
Is to fight and fight and fight.

We will have to join the union,
They will help you find a way
How to get a better living
And for your work get better pay.

*Lyrics by Sarah Ogan Gunning. © Copyright 1965
by Folk-Legacy Records. Used by permission.*

## Detroit City

Last night I went to sleep in Detroit City
And I dreamed about the cotton fields and home
I dreamed about my mother, dear old papa, sister and brother
And I dreamed about the girl who's been waiting for so long.

I wanna go home, I wanna go home
Oh, how I wanna go home.

Home folks think I'm big in Detroit City
From the letters that I write they think I'm fine
But by day I make the cars, by night I make the bars
If only they could read between the lines.

'Cause you know I rode a freight train north to Detroit City
And after all these years I find I've just been wasting my time
So I'll just take my foolish pride and put it on the Southbound freight and ride
And go back to the loved ones, the ones that I left waiting so far behind.

*By Danny Dill and Mel Tillis. © Copyright 1963
Used with permission of Cedarwood Publishing Co., Inc.*

## CHAPTER 4

### San Quentin

San Quentin, you've been livin' hell to me,
You've hosted me since 1963.
I've seen 'em come and go, and I've seen 'em die
And long ago, I stopped askin' why.

San Quentin, I hate every inch of you.
You've cut me and have scarred me through and through
And I'll walk out a wiser, weaker man.
Mr. Congressman, you can't understand.

San Quentin, what good do you think you do?
Do you think I'll be different when you're through?
You bent my heart and mind, and you've warped my soul
And your stone walls turn my blood a little cold.

San Quentin, may you rot and burn in Hell,
May your walls fall and may I live to tell,
May all the world forget you ever stood
And may all the world regret you did no good.

San Quentin, I hate every inch of you.

### What Is Truth?

The old man turned off the radio
Said, "Where did all of the old songs go?
Kids sure play funny music these days;
They play it in the strangest ways."
Said, "It looks to me like they've all gone wild,
It was peaceful back when I was a child."
Well man could it be that girls and boys
Are tryin' to be heard above your noise?
And the lonely voice of youth cries
What is truth?

A little boy of three sittin' on the floor
Looks up and says, "Daddy, what is war?"

"Son, that's when people fight and die."
A little boy of three says, "Daddy, why?"
Young man of 17 in Sunday school
Being taught the Golden Rule
And by the time another year's gone around
It may be his turn to lay his life down.
Can you blame the voice of youth for asking
What is truth?

Young man sitting on a witness stand
The man with the Book says, "Raise your hand,
Repeat after me, 'I solemnly swear,'"
The man looked down at his long hair
And although the young man solemnly swore
Nobody seemed to hear any more
And it didn't really matter if the truth was there
It was the cut of his clothes and the length of his hair
And the lonely voice of youth cries
What is truth?

The young girl dancin' to the latest beat
Has found new ways to move her feet.
The young man speakin' on the city square
Is trying to tell somebody that he cares.
Yeah, the ones that you're callin' wild
Are gonna be the leaders in a little while.
This old world's wakin' to a new born day
And I solemnly swear it'll be their way.
You better help that voice of youth find
What is truth.

And the lonely voice of youth cries
What is truth?

**Man In Black**

Well, you wonder why I always dress in black,
Why you never see bright colors on my back,
And why does my appearance seem to have a somber tone?
Well, there's a reason for the things that I have on.

Ah, I wear the black for the poor and the beaten down,
Livin' in the hopeless, hungry side of town,
I wear the black for the prisoner who has long paid for his crime,
But is there because he's a victim of the times.

I wear black for those who never read,
Or listened to the words that Jesus said,
About the road to happiness thru love and charity,
Why, you'd think He's talking straight to you and me.
Ah, we're doin' mighty fine, I do suppose,
In our streak of lightnin' cars and fancy clothes,
But just so we're reminded of the ones who are held back,
Up there in front oughta be a Man in Black.

I wear it for the sick and the lonely old,
For the reckless ones whose bad trip left them cold
I wear the black in mournin' for the lives that could have been,
Each week we lose a hundred fine young men.
Ah, I wear it for the thousands who have died,
Believin' that the Lord was on their side,
And I wear it for another hundred thousand who have died,
Believin' that we all were on their side.

Well, there's things that never will be right I know
And things need changin' everywhere you go,
But until we start to make a move to make a few things right,
You'll never see me in a suit of white.
Oh, I'd love to wear a rainbow every day,
And tell the world that everything's OK,
But I'll try to carry off a little darkness on my back,
Till things are brighter, I'm the Man in Black.

*By John R. Cash. © Copyright 1971 House of Cash, Inc.*
*Used by permission. All rights reserved.*

**Ragged Old Flag**

I walked through a county courthouse square,
On a park bench an old man was sitting there.
I said, "Your old courthouse is kinda run down."
He said, "Naw, it'll do for our little town."
I said, "Your old flagpole has leaned a little bit,
And that's a Ragged Old Flag you got hanging on it."

He said, "Have a seat," and I sat down.
"Is this the first time you've been to our little town?"
I said, "I think it is." He said, "I don't like to brag,
But we're kinda proud of that Ragged Old Flag.

"You see, we got a little hole in that flag there
When Washington took it across the Delaware.
And it got powder-burned the night Francis Scott Key
Sat watching it writing Say Can You See.
And it got a bad rip in New Orleans
With Packingham and Jackson tuggin' at its seams.

"And it almost fell at the Alamo
Beside the Texas flag, but she waved on though.
She got cut with a sword at Chancellorsville
And she got cut again at Shiloh Hill.
There was Robert E. Lee, Beauregard, and Bragg,
And the south wind blew hard on that Ragged Old Flag.

"On Flanders Field in World War I
She got a big hole from a Bertha gun.
She turned blood red in World War II.
She hung limp and low by the time it was through.
She was in Korea and Vietnam.
She went where she was sent by her Uncle Sam.
She waved from our ships upon the briny foam,
And now they've about quit waving her back here at home.
In her own good land here she's been abused—
She's been burned, dishonored, denied, and refused.

"And the government for which she stands
Is scandalized throughout the land.
And she's getting threadbare and wearing thin,
But she's in good shape for the shape she's in.
'Cause she's been through the fire before
And I believe she can take a whole lot more.

"So we raise her up every morning, take her down every night.
We don't let her touch the ground and we fold her up right.
On second thought I do like to brag,
'Cause I'm mighty proud of that Ragged Old Flag."

## CHAPTER 5

### Busted

My bills are all due, and the baby needs shoes
But I'm busted
Cotton is down to a quarter a pound
And I'm busted
I got a cow that went dry and a hen that won't lay
A big stack of bills that gets bigger each day
The county's gonna haul my belongings away
'Cause I'm busted.

I went to my brother to ask for a loan
'Cause I was busted
I hate to beg like a dog for a bone
But I'm busted
My brother said, "There ain't a thing I can do
My wife and my kids are all down with the flu
And I was just thinking about callin' on you
'Cause I'm busted."

Well, I am no thief, but a man can go wrong
When he's busted
The food that we canned last summer is gone
And I'm busted
The fields are all bare, and the cotton won't grow
Me and my family got to pack up and go
But I'll make a living, just where I don't know
'Cause I'm busted.

### Gentle On My Mind

It's knowing that your door is always open and your path is free to walk
That makes me tend to leave my sleeping bag rolled up and stashed behind
  your couch
And it's knowing I'm not shackled by forgotten words and bonds and the ink
  stains that have dried upon some line

That keeps you in the back roads, by the rivers of my mem'ry that keeps you
ever gentle on my mind.

It's not clinging to the rocks and ivy planted on their columns now that bind me
Or something that somebody said because they thought we fit together
walkin'
It's just knowing that the world will not be cursing or forgiving
When I walk along some railroad track and find
That you're moving on the back roads, by the rivers of my mem'ry
And for hours, you're just gentle on my mind.

Though the wheat fields and the clothes lines and the junkyards and the
highways come between us
And some other woman's crying to her mother 'cause she turned and I was
gone
I still run in silence, tears of joy might stain my face
And summer sun might burn me 'til I'm blind
But not to where I cannot see you walkin' on the back roads
By the rivers flowing gentle on my mind.

I dip my cup of soup back from the gurglin' cracklin' caldron in some train yard
My beard a roughening coal pile and a dirty hat pulled low across my face
Through cupped hands 'round a tin can
I pretend I hold you to my breast and find
That you're waving from the back roads, by the rivers of my mem'ry
Ever smilin', ever gentle on my mind.

## San Francisco Mabel Joy

Lord, his daddy was an honest man—just a red dirt Georgia farmer.
His mama lived her short life havin' kids and bailin' hay.
He had fifteen years and he ached inside to wander.
He jumped a freight in Waycross and wound up in L.A.

Cold nights had no pity on that Waycross, Georgia farmboy.
Most days he went hungry and then the summer came.
He met a girl known on the strip as San Francisco's Mabel Joy.
Destitution's child born of an L.A. street called shame.

Growin' up came quietly in the arms of Mabel Joy.
Laughter found their mornin's. It brought a meanin' to his life.

Lord, on the night before she left, sleep came and left that country boy
With dreams of Georgia cotton and a California wife.

Sunday mornin' found him standin' 'neath the red light at her door.
A right-cross sent him reelin', put his face down on the floor.
In place of his Mabel Joy, he found a merchant, mad marine,
Who growled, "Your Georgia neck is red, but sonny you're still green."

He turned twenty-one in a grey, rock, Federal prison.
The old judge had no mercy on that Waycross, Georgia, boy.
Starin' at those four grey walls in silence, Lord, he just listened
To the midnight freight he knew could take him back to Mabel Joy.

Sunday mornin' found him lyin' 'neath the red light at her door.
With a bullet in his side he cried, "Have you seen Mabel Joy?"
Stunned and shaken, someone said, "Son, she don't live here no more.
No, she left this house four years, today, They say she's lookin' for
Some Georgia farm boy."

**Ride Me Down Easy**

The highway she's a-hotter
Than nine kinds of hell;
Rides they're as scarce as the rain;
When you're down to your last shuck
With nothin' to sell
And too far away from the trains.

Been a good month of Sundays
And a guitar ago,
Had a tall drink of yesterday's wine;
Left a long string of friends,
Some sheets in the wind
And some satisfied women behind.

Ride me down easy, Lord
Ride me on down;
Leave word in the dust where I lay.
Say I'm easy come, easy go,
And easy to love when I stay

Put snow on the mountain,
Raised hell on the hill;
Locked horns with the devil himself;
Been a rodeo bum
A son of a gun
And a hobo with stars in my crown.

Ride me down easy, Lord
Ride me on down;
Leave word in the dust where I lay.
Say I'm easy come, easy go,
And easy to love when I stay.

## Where Have All Our Heroes Gone?

Where have all our heroes gone?
What's come over our great land
America is still my home, sweet home
But where have all our heroes gone?

*Recitation:*

I saw a group of boys the other day, standing in a corner of a playground, looking and laughing at a magazine; and I overheard one of the boys say, "Man, is he ever cool." And he pointed to the man whose picture was on the magazine cover. And everybody kinda said under their breath, "Yeah, he's cool, all right." And I got sick to my stomach, because I'd seen the cover, and the "man" that they were talkin' about had instigated a riot in one of our major cities last summer. And the magazine was writing about how the police were unkind to him, the judges were unfair with him, and how he talked back and slung his long hair about, and cussed and did his thing. And they made him into a regular hero. And inside this magazine was the story of the baseball player who got involved with the gamblers. Of the football player who said that football was not the end, just a means to an end, meaning the girls and the good times. And a story of the folk singer who proudly claims to be both a member of a party alien to our government and a non-tax-paying citizen. These young boys read with open eyes and open minds. And I thought to myself, "My God, are these the people that these young boys look up to? Are these their idols? Are these the heroes of the Now Generation?" I had heroes when I was a kid.

We all did. And our heroes did their thing, too. Like General Douglas MacArthur, who returned like he said he would. Like Gene Autry and Roy Rogers, who chased the bad guys right off the screen. Like Lindbergh, who flew the ocean, and Jesse Owens, who showed Hitler, and John Wayne and Gary Cooper. After all, didn't they really win the war? And General Ike, bless your soul, 'cause you made us feel safe. We've killed some of our recent heroes—the Kennedys, the Kings. And, even as great as their space feats are, how many of the astronauts can you name? Huh? How many? My heroes were people like Joe DiMaggio, who proved that nice guys can finish first, and Stan Musial, who never had an unkind word for anybody. And Winston Churchill, whose two fingers raised together meant victory, not just a let-your-enemy-have-it-all kind of artificial peace. This country needs a lot of things today, friends. But it doesn't need any one thing any more than it needs some real heroes. Men who know what it means to be looked up to by a grimy-faced kid. Men who want to sign autograph books and not deals under the table. Men who are willing to play the game with the people who made them heroes. Men who don't mind putting on a white hat and saying "thank you" and "please." I wish I knew just one man that I'd be proud for my son to look up to and say, "Daddy, when I grow up, I want to be just like him."

## Outside the Nashville City Limits

Outside the Nashville city limits
A friend and I did drive
On a day in early winter
I was glad to be alive.

We went to see some friends of his
Who lived upon a farm
Strange and gentle country folk
Who wished nobody harm
Fresh-cut sixty acres
Eight cows in the barn.

But the thing that I remember
On that cold day in December
Was that my eyes they did brim over
As we talked.

In the slowest drawl I've ever heard
The man said come with me
If ya'll wanna see the prettiest place

In all of Tennessee.

He poured us each a glass of wine
And a-walking we did go
Along fallen leaves and crackling ice
Where a tiny brook did flow
He knew every inch of the land
And Lord he loved it so.

But the thing that I remember
On that cold day in December
Was that my eyes were brimming over
As we walked.

He set me down upon a stone
Beside a running spring
He talked in a voice so soft and clear
Like the waters I heard sing.

He said we searched quite a time
For a place to call our own
There was jsut me and Mary John
And now I guess we're home
I looked at the ground and wondered
How many years they each had roamed.

And Lord I do remember
On that cold day late December
How my eyes kept brimming over
As we talked.

And standing there with outstretched arms
He said to me, you know
I can't wait til the heavy storms
Cover the ground with snow.

And there on the pond the water-cress
Is all that don't turn white
When the sun is high you squint your eyes
And look at the hills so bright
And nodding his head my friend said
It seems like overnight
That the leaves come out so tender
At the turning of the winter.
I thought the skies they would brim over
As we talked.

## Sweet Sunny South

*Chorus:*
Take me back to the place where I first saw the light
To my sweet sunny South take me home
Where the wild birds sing me to sleep every night
Oh why was I tempted to roam?

The path to our cabin they say has grown green
And the stones are quite mossy around
And I know that the faces and forms that I love
Now lie in the cold mossy ground.

*Repeat chorus.*

Take me back to the place where the orange trees grow
To my place in the evergreen shade
Where the flowers on the river's green margin do grow
And share their sweet scent with the glade.

Take me back to the place where I first saw the light
To my sweet sunny South take me home
Where the wild birds sing me to sleep every night
Oh why was I tempted to roam?

*Traditional (as sung by Joan Baez and Jeffrey Shurtleff)*
*Vanguard Records*

# CHAPTER 6

## White Man Singing the Blues

The old man paid no mind to color
'Cause he knew that I'd been down and out
Old Joe said that I was a soul brother
From things I'd been singin' about
He liked how I played my old guitar
He sat down beside me to sing
Together we hummed out an old-timey blues

On the same side of the railroad track
Where people have nothing to lose
I'm the son of a gambler whose luck never came
And a white man singing the blues

We both done a heap o' hard livin'
And hard to describe in a song
But the blues was one thing we both understood
And the old man hummed right along

On the same side of the railroad track
Where people have nothing to lose
I'm the son of a gambler whose luck never came
And a white man singing the blues

### Cortelia Clark

I was just a boy the year the Bluebird Special came through here
On its first run south to New Orleans.
A blind old man and I, we came to Guthrie just to see the train.
He was black and I was green.

"Tell me what you see," he said. "Is the engine black or red,
Son that's the loudest thing I've ever seen."
Then he picked his guitar up, sat on the fender of the truck
And his eyes lit up as he began to sing.

And I remember when that old man's dreams were chained
To a depot down in the Guthrie and a Bluebird Special train.

He picked his guitar up, shuffled down the walk
The cars uptown wound round the buildings at his feet.
Lookin' mighty proud, that old man, with his battered hat in his hand
Lord he sung a song that made me weep. Yes, he made me weep.

I read it in a week old paper, no one made it for his wake
Or laid a flower at his feet.
'He was just a blind old beggar,' people said, but, Lord, I'll wager
He won't be beggin' up there on your streets.

And you'll find him, Lord, this mornin', he'll be steppin' from the dark.
Can you save a street in glory, Lord, for Cortelia Clark?

I was just a boy the year the Bluebird Special came through here
On its first run south to New Orleans.
A blind old man and I, we came to Guthrie just to see the train.
He was black and was I green.

## Catfish John

Let me dream of another mornin'
And a time so long ago
When the sweet magnolias blossomed
Cotton fields were white as snow

Catfish John was a river hobo
And he lived by the river bend
Thinkin' back I still remember
I was proud to be his friend

Mama said don't go near that river
Don't go hangin' round ol' Catfish John
But come the mornin' I'd always be there
Walkin' in his footsteps in the sweet delta dawn

Born a slave in the town of Vicksburg
Traded for a chestnut mare
Still he never spoke in anger
Though his load was hard to bear

*By Bob McDill & Allen Reynolds. © Copyright 1972 Jack Music, Inc.*
*Used by permission. All rights reserved.*

## Rednecks, White Socks and Blue Ribbon Beer

The barmaid is mad cause some guy made a pass
The jukebox is playin' "There Stands the Glass"
And the cigarette smoke kinda hangs in the air
Rednecks, white socks and Blue Ribbon Beer

A cowboy is cussin' the pinball machine
A drunk at the bar is gettin' noisy and mean
And some guy on the phone says "I'll be home soon dear"
Rednecks, white socks and Blue Ribbon Beer

No we don't fit in with that white collar crowd
We're a little too rowdy and a little too loud
But there's no place that I'd rather be than right here
With my red neck, white socks and Blue Ribbon Beer

The semis are passing on the highway outside
The 4:30 crowd is about to arrive

The sun's goin' down and we'll soon all be here
Rednecks, white socks and Blue Ribbon Beer
No we don't fit in with that white collar crowd
We're a little too rowdy and a little too loud
But there's no place that I'd rather be than right here
With my red neck, white socks and Blue Ribbon Beer

*By Bob McDill, Wayland Holyfield and Chuck Neese. © Copyright*
*Jack Music, Inc. All rights reserved. Used by permission.*

## I Believe the South Is Gonna Rise Again

Mama never had a flower garden
Cause cotton grew right up to our front door
Daddy never went on a vacation
He died a tired old man at forty-four

Our neighbors in the big house called us "redneck"
Cause we lived in a poor sharecropper shack
The Jacksons down the road were poor like we were
But our skin was white and theirs was black

But I believe the South is gonna rise again
And not the way we thought it would back then
I mean everybody hand in hand
I believe the South is gonna rise again

I see wooded parks and big skyscrapers
Where once stood red clay hills and cottonfields
I see sons and daughters of sharecroppers
Drinking scotch and making business deals

But more important I see human progress
As we forget the bad and keep the good
A brand new breeze is blowing cross the Southland
And I see a brand new kind of brotherhood

Yes, I believe the South is gonna rise again
But not the way we thought it would back then
I mean everybody hand in hand
I believe the South is gonna rise again

*Words and music by Bobby Braddock. © Copyright 1973*
*by Tree Publishing Co., Inc. International copyright secured*

## The Family Way

I cried bitter teardrops all the way to Doc Johnson's office
He said, "I won't come, you'll have to go and get the midwife."
So I ran barefooted through the ankle-deep snow to fetch Aunt Elly Mae Jones
And I thought, Lord, how come a human has to live such a dog's life

*Bridge:*
Brother's in jail for making whiskey, and Mama's in the family way
And Daddy's been dead one year ago today
Daddy's been dead one year ago today

Aunt Elly Mae came to the door, but I couldn't talk for my teeth a'chattering
She said, "Lord's sake, young'un, get over there by the fireside."
She was bent 'n old, but I needed a friend, and to her that's all that mattered
For she held me close and soothed my tears when I cried

*Repeat bridge.*

She went to the kitchen and brought me a cup of coffee and side meat bacon
She said, "Be quick about eating, we'd better hurry."
So we left right shortly and got back to my house just as day was breaking
She said, "Heat me up some water, boy, don't you worry."

*Repeat bridge.*

Two hours later, my Mama gave birth to my nameless baby brother
I walked the floor and prayed to the Lord I could die
Aunt Elly Mae said, "Now, don't be harboring bad thoughts toward your
    mother
A human is a human and a saint's mighty hard to come by."

Go tell the jailer to fetch your brother, cause your Mama just passed away
I just don't know why things have to happen this way
But the good Lord's gonna straighten everything out someday.

*Words and music by Don Wayne. © Copyright 1974*
*by Tree Publishing Company, Inc. International copyright secured.*


## Memories of Us

The old man who sold his apples
Isn't there anymore
And the city square don't seem as big
As it did before
They tore down that old drug store
We used to love so much
But everything is still the same

In my memories of us

That old school bus has long stopped running
And I heard the driver died
And the movie house is all boarded up
Where we sat side by side
And the sign that said state champions
It's covered up with dust
But everything is still the same
In my memories of us

In my memories of us
Things are still the same
For yesterdays are something
Tomorrows cannot change
For freckles just don't disappear
And pigtails never rust
And everything is still the same
In my memories of us

*Words and music by Dave Kirby and Glenn Martin. © Copyright 1975*
*by Tree Publishing Co., Inc. International copyright secured.*

## New York City Song

I'm sittin' in this New York City hotel room alone
Wishin' I was somewhere else or on my way back home.
Nashville, Tennessee I know that's where I belong
Cause I don't know no New York City song.

They know I'm from Dixie when I open up my mouth
And they don't treat the ladies here the way they do down South.
I thought I could make it here but I can't get along
Cause I don't know no New York City song.

And Lord I'd like to tell you just how much I'd like to leave
Cause in my mind that southbound song is tuggin' on my sleeve.
New York City ain't the place a country girl should be
No, New York City ain't the place for me.

Today I walked a New York City avenue downtown.
I've never seen so many people hurryin' around
And when I smile they look as if to say that smilin's wrong.
No, I don't know no New York City song.

*By Linda Hargrove. © 1972 Tomake Music Co., Inc.*
*Used by permission. All rights reserved.*

CHAPTER 7

## You've Never Been This Far Before

I can almost hear the stillness
As it yields to the sound of your heart beating
And I can almost hear the echo of the thoughts I know you must be thinking
And I can feel your body tremble
As you wonder what this moment holds in store
And as I put my arms around you, I can tell
You've never been this far before.

I don't know what I'm saying
As my trembling fingers touch forbidden places
I only know that I've waited for so long
For the chance that we are taking
I don't know and I don't care
What made you tell him you don't love him anymore
And as I taste your tender kisses, I can tell
You've never been this far before.

And as I take the love you're giving
I can feel the tension building in your mind
And you're wond'ring if tomorrow
I'll still love you like I'm loving you tonight.
You have no way of knowing
But tonight will only make me love you more
And I hope that you'll believe me
Cause I know, you've never been this far before.

*Words and music by Conway Twitty. © Copyright 1973
by Twitty Bird Music Publishing Co.
Used by permission. International copyright secured.*

## Don't Come Home A-Drinkin'

Well, you thought I'd be waitin' up when you came home last night
You'd been out with all the boys, and you ended up half tight
But liquor and love they just don't mix; leave the bottle or me behind
And don't come home a-drinkin' with lovin' on your mind.

No, don't come home a-drinkin' with lovin' on your mind
Just stay out on the town and see what you can find
'Cause if you want that kind of love,
Well, you don't need none of mine
So don't come home a-drinkin' with lovin' on your mind.

You never take me anywhere, because you're always gone
And many a night I've laid awake and cried there all alone
Then you come in a-kissin' on me, it happens every time
So don't come home a-drinkin' with lovin' on your mind.

*By Loretta Lynn.* © *Copyright 1966*
*Used with permission of Sure-Fire Music Co., Inc.*

## One's On the Way

They say to have her hair done Liz flies all the way to France
And Jackie's seen in a discotheque doin' a brand new dance
And the White House social season should be glittering and gay
But here in Topeka
The rain is afallin'
The faucet is adrippin'
And the kids are abrawlin'
One of them atoddlin' and one is acrawlin'
And one's on the way.

I'm glad that Raquel Welch just signed a million dollar pact
And Debbie's out in Vegas workin' up a brand new act
While the TV's showin' newly weds a real fun game to play
But here in Topeka
The screen door's abangin'
The coffee's boilin' over
And the wash needs ahangin'
One wants a cookie and one wants a changin'
And one's on the way.

Now what was I doin?
Jimmy get away from there,
Darn, there goes the phone.
Hello honey, what's that you say?

## WATERMELON WINE
### 222

You're bringin' a few old army buddies home?
You're callin' from a bar?
Get away from there.
No, not you honey, I was talking to the baby,
Wait a minute honey the doorbell.
Honey, could you stop at the market and...hello,
Hello, well I'll be...

The girls in New York City, they all march for women's lib
And Better Homes and Gardens shows the modern way to live
And the pill may change the world tomorrow, but meanwhile today
Here in Topeka
The flies are abuzzin'
The dog is abarkin' and
The floor needs a scrubbin'
One needs a spankin' and
One needs a huggin'
And one's on the way.

*Words and music by Shel Silverstein. © Copyright 1971
Evil Eye Music, Inc., New York, N.Y. Used by permission.*

## The Pill

You wined me and dined me when I was your girl,
Promised if I'd be your wife you'd show me the world,
But all I've seen of this old world is a bed and a doctor bill
I'm tearin' down your brooder house 'cause now I've got the Pill.

All these years I've stayed at home while you had all your fun,
And every year that's gone by another baby's come.
There's gonna be some changes made right here on Nurs'ry Hill,
You've set this chicken your last time, 'cause now I've got the Pill.

This old maternity dress I've got is goin' in the garbage.
The clothes I'm wearin' from now on won't take up so much yardage!
Mini skirts and hot pants with a few little fancy frills,
Yeah, I'm makin' up for all those years since I've got the Pill.

I'm tired of all your crowin' 'bout how you and your hens play,
While holdin' a couple in my arms and another's on the way.

This chicken's done tore up her nest and I'm ready to make a deal,
And you can't afford to turn it down 'cause you know I've got the Pill.

This incubator is over used because you kept it filled,
The feeling good comes easy now since I've got the Pill!
It's gettin' dark, it's roosting time, tonight's too good to be real,
And Daddy don't you worry none, 'cause Mama's got the Pill.

## Instant Coffee Blues

He washed all the road dirt from his face and from his neck
And sat down at her table and she picked up his check
And she took him home for reasons that she did not understand
And him he had the answers but did not play his hand
For him he knew the taste of this wine very well
It all goes down so easy but the next day is hell
"Morning."
"Man was I drunk," she whispered in the shower
While he lay there and smoked his way there through the final hour
And she felt wholly empty like she'd felt it every time
And he was feelin' just the same 'cept he's trying to make it rhyme
Time was of the essence so they both did their best
To meet up in the kitchen feelin' fully dressed
And she just had to go to work and he just had to go
And she knew where and he knew how to blow it off and so
They shot the breeze quite cavalier to the boilin' of the pot
And sing the Instant Coffee Blues and never fired a shot
And him he hit the driveway with his feelin's in a case
And her she hit the stoplight and touched up her face
So you tell them the difference between caring and not
And that it's all done with mirrors lest they forgot
I said it's all done with mirrors of which they have none
To blend the Instant Coffee Blues into the morning sun

## CHAPTER 8

### This World Is Not My Home

This world is not my home, I'm just a-passing through
My treasures are laid up somewhere beyond the blue
The angels beckon me from heaven's open door
And I can't feel at home in this world anymore.

*Traditional*

### I Saw The Light

I saw the light, I saw the light
No more darkness, no more night
Now I'm so happy, no sorrow in sight
Praise the Lord! I saw the light.

I wandered so aimless, life filled with sin
I wouldn't let my dear Saviour in
Then Jesus came like a stranger in the night
Praise the Lord! I saw the light.

Just like a blind man, I wandered alone
Worries and fears I claimed for my own
Then like a blind man that God gave back his sight
Praise the Lord! I saw the light.

*By Hank Williams. © Copyright 1948 Renewed 1975*
*Fred Rose Music, Inc. Used by permission of the publisher. All rights reserved.*

### Country Bumpkin

His big round ears were stickin' out beneath the straw hat resting on his head.
His honest face was weathered and his nose was a shiny sunburned red.
He was dressed in clean-pressed duckhead overalls and a shirt of faded blue.
You could look at him and almost smell the barnyard on his scuffed-up brogan
   shoes.

He walked into a bar and parked his lanky frame upon a tall barstool
And with a long soft souther drawl said "I'll just have a glass of anything that's
   cool."
A barroom girl with wise and knowing eyes slowly looked him up and down

And she thought "I wonder how on earth that country bumpkin found his way to town."

And she said "Hello country bumpkin, how's the frost out on the pumpkins?
I've seen some sights, but boy, you're somethin'! Where'd you come from, country bumpkin?"

Just a short year later in a sweat-drenched bed of joy and tears and death-like pain
Into this wondrous world of many wonders, one more wonder came.
That same woman's face was wrapped up in a raptured look of love and tenderness
As she marvelled at the soft and warm and cuddly boy-child suckin' at her breast.

And she said "Hello country bumpkin, fresh as frost out on the pumpkins,
I've seen some sights, but babe, you're somethin'! Mama loves her country bumpkin."

Forty years of hard work later, in a simple quiet and peaceful country place
The heavy hand of time had not erased the raptured wonder from the woman's face.
She was lying in her death bed knowing fully well her race was nearly run
But she softly smiled and looked up at the sad eyes of her husband and her son.

And she said, "So long country bumpkins, the frost is gone now from the pumpkins.
I've seen some sights, and life's been somethin'. See you later, country bumpkins."

## The Seeker

I am the seeker
Poor sinful creature
There is none weaker than I am
I am a seeker
And you are a teacher
You are a rancher so reach down
Reach out and lead me
Guide me and keep me
In the shelter of your care each day

Cause I am a seeker
And you are a keeper
You are a leader
Won't you show me the way
I am a vessel that's empty and useless
I am a bad seed that fell by the way
I am a loser that wants to be a winner
You are my last hope don't turn me away

I am a seeker
A poor sinful creature
There is none weaker than I am
I am a seeker
And you are a teacher
You are a reacher so reach down
Reach out and lead me
Guide me and keep me
In the shelter of your care every day

Cause I am a seeker
And you are a keeper
You are a leader won't you show me the way

You are a mountain from which there comes a fountain
So let its water wash my sins away
Cause I am a seeker
And you are a keeper
You are a teacher won't you teach me the way
Reach out and lead me
Guide me and keep me
In the shelter of your care each day.

*By Dolly Parton. © Copyright Owepar Publishing Co.*
*Used by permission. All rights reserved.*

## Keep Me From Blowing Away

I've spent my whole lifetime
In a world where the sunshine
Found excuses for not stayin' round.
I've squandered my emotions
On the slightest of notions
On the first easy woman I found.
But soon all the good times,

The gay times and the play times
Like colors run together and fade.
Oh Lord, if you hear me,
Touch me and hold me
And keep me from blowing away.

There's times when I tremble
When my mind remembers
The days that just crumbled away.
With nothing to show
But these lines that I know
Are beginning to show in my face.
Oh Lord, if you're list'nin'
I know I'm no Christian
And I ain't got much comin' to me
But send down some sunshine
Throw out the lifeline
And keep me from blowing away.

## Rosalie's Good Eats Cafe

It's two in the morning on Saturday night
At Rosalie's Good Eats Cafe
The onions are fryin', the neon is bright
And the juke box is startin' to play
And the sign on the wall says In God We Trust
All others have to pay
And it's two in the morning on Saturday night
At Rosalie's Good Eats Cafe

The short order cook with the Mama tattoo
Is a-turnin' them hamburgers slow
The eggs over easy, whole wheat down
Do y'all want that coffee to go
He never once dreamed as a rodeo star
That he'd wind up here today
At two in the morning on Saturday night
At Rosalie's Good Eats Cafe

There's a tall skinny girl in the booth in the back
Wearing jeans and a second-hand fur

# WATERMELON WINE

She's been to the doctor and called up "a" man
And now wonders just where she can turn
She stares at her coffee and looks toward the ceiling
But Lord, it's a strange place to pray
At two in the morning on Saturday night
At Rosalie's Good Eats Cafe

There's a guy in a tux and he stands in the corner
Feedin' the juke box his dimes
He just had a woman and thought that he'd bought her
But found he'd just rented some time
And he couldn't sleep so he came back to see
If anyone else wants to play
At two in the morning on Saturday night
At Rosalie's Good Eats Cafe

Now there's an old dollar bill in a frame on the wall
The first one that Rose ever made
It was once worth a dollar a long time ago
But like Rose it's startin' to fade
She's back of the register dreamin' of someone
And how things'd be if he'd stayed
But it's two in the morning on Saturday night
At Rosalie's Good Eats Cafe

The stoop-shouldered man and his frizzy-haired woman
It's strange how their eyes never meet
He's playin' the pinball, she's fixin' the blanket
Of the baby asleep on the seat
He's out of work, she's puttin' on weight
And they never did have too much to say
It's two in the morning on Saturday night
At Rosalie's Good Eats Cafe

The waitress Darlene, she sits at the counter
Paintin' her fingernails blue
And the short order cook he yells move it or lose it
And pick up an order of stew
But someday a rich handsome man will walk in
And carry her far, far away
From two in the morning on Saturday night
At Rosalie's Good Eats Cafe

The shaggy-haired hippy, he's finished his meal
And he's countin' the change in his jeans
Burger and coffee are 85 cents

And he's only got 23
But he smiles at Rose and she winks back at him
But Lord it's a high price to pay
At two in the morning on Saturday night
At Rosalie's Good Eats Cafe

The baby-faced sailor he leans on the phone
And dials the number again
While the guy in the tux tells the girl in the jeans
'Bout the wonderful places he's been
And the wino comes in off the street and starts shoutin'
'Bout fortunes that he threw away
And Rosalie's askin' the shaggy-haired hippy
If he's got a warm place to stay
And the short order cook takes a five from the till
While Rosalie's lookin' away
And the onions keep fryin', the neon is bright
And the juke box continues to play
And it's two in the morning on Saturday night
At Rosalie's Good Eats Cafe

## CHAPTER 9

### Blue Eyes Crying in the Rain

In the twilight glow I see her
Blue eyes crying in the rain
When we kissed goodbye and parted
I knew we'd never meet again

Love is like a dying ember
And only memories remain
Through the ages I'll remember
Blue eyes crying in the rain

Someday when we meet up yonder
We'll stroll hand in hand again
In a land that knows no parting
Blue eyes crying in the rain

## It's Not For Me To Understand

I passed a home the other day
The yard was filled with kids at play
And on the sidewalk of this home
A little boy stood all alone.

His smiling face was sweet and kind
And I could see the boy was blind
He listened to the children play
I bowed my head and there I prayed.

Dear Lord above, why must this be?
And then these words came down to me
After all you're just a man
And it's not for you to understand.
It's not for you to reason why
You, too, are blind without my eyes
So question not what I command
It's not for you to understand.

Now when I pray my prayer is one
I pray his will, not mine be done
For after all I'm just a man
And it's not for me to understand.

## Desperados Waiting for the Train

I'd play the Red River Valley
And he'd sit in the kitchen and cry
And run his fingers through 70 years of livin'
And wonder Lord, has every well I drilled run dry
We was friends me and this old man
Like desperados waiting for the train
Like desperados waiting for the train

He's a drifter and a driller of oil wells
And an old school man of the world
He taught me how to drive his car when he's too drunk to
And he'd wink and give me money for the girls
And our lives was like some old western movie

Like desperados waiting for the train
Like desperados waiting for the train

From the time that I could walk he'd take me with him
To a bar called the Green Frog Cafe
And there was old men with beer guts and dominoes
Lyin' bout their lives while they'd play
And I was just a kid they all called his sidekick
Like desperados waiting for the train
Like desperados waiting for the train

One day I looked up and he's pushing 80
And there's brown tobacco stains all down his chin
To me he's one of the heroes of this country
So why's he all dressed up like them old men
Drinkin' beer and playin' Moon & 42
Like a desperado waiting for the train
Like a desperado waiting for the train

The day before he died I went to see him
I was grown and he was almost gone
So we just closed our eyes and dreamed us up a kitchen
And sang another verse of that old song
Come on Jack, that son of a bitch is coming
And we're desperados waiting for the train
Desperados waiting for the train.

*By Guy Clark. © Copyright 1973 by Sunbury Music, Inc.*
*Used by permission. All rights reserved.*

# CHAPTER 10

## The South's Gonna Do It

Well, the train to Grinderswitch is runnin' right on time
And the Tucker boys are cookin' down in Caroline.
People down in Florida can't be still
When ol' Lynard Skynard's pickin' down in Jacksonville.
People down in Georgia come from near and far
To hear Richard Betts pickin' on his red guitar.

So gather round, gather round children,
Get down. Well, just get down children,
Get loud. Well you can be loud and be proud,

And you can be proud here, be proud to a rebel
Cause the South's gonna do it again.

Elvin Bishop's sittin' on a bale of hay
He ain't good lookin' but he sure can play.
And there's ZZ Top and you can't forget
That old brother Willy's gettin' soakin' wet.
And all the good people down in Tennessee
Are diggin' Barefoot Jerry and the CDB.

So gather round, gather round children,
Get down. Well, just get down children,
Get loud. Well you can be loud and be proud,
And you can be proud here, be proud to a rebel
Cause the South's gonna do it again.

## Long Haired Country Boy

People say I'm no good and crazy as a loon,
'Cause I get stoned in the morning, I get drunk in the afternoon.
Kinda like my old blue tick hound, I like to lay around in the shade.
And I ain't got no money, but I damn sure got it made.
And I ain't askin' nobody for nothin', if I can't get it on my own.
If you don't like the way I'm livin',
You just leave this long haired country boy alone.

Preacher man talkin' on TV, puttin' down the rock and roll,
Wants me to send a donation, 'cause he's worried about my soul.
He said Jesus walked on the water, and I know that it's true,
But sometimes I think that preacher man would like to do a little walking, too.
But I ain't askin' nobody for nothin', if I can't get it on my own.
If you don't like the way I'm livin',
You just leave this long haired country boy alone.

A poor girl wants to marry, and a rich girl wants to flirt;
A rich man goes to college, and a poor man goes to work;
A drunkard wants another drink of wine, and the politician wants the vote;
I don't want much of nothin' at all, but I will take another toke.
But I ain't askin' nobody for nothin', if I can't get it on my own.

If you don't like the way I'm livin',
You just leave this long haired country boy alone.

## Bye Bye Love

There goes my baby with someone new;
She sure looks happy, I sure am blue;
She was my baby till he stepped in;
Goodbye to romance that might have been.

Bye bye love: bye bye happiness;
Hello loneliness—I think I'm gonna cry;
Bye bye love; bye bye sweet caress;
Hello emptiness; I feel like I could die.

I'm through with romance, I'm through with love.
I'm through with counting the stars above;
And here's the reason that I'm so free:
My lovin' baby is through with me.

Bye bye love: bye bye happiness;
Hello loneliness—I think I'm gonna cry;
Bye bye love; bye bye sweet caress;
Hello emptiness; I feel like I could die.

## CHAPTER 11

## Can The Circle Be Unbroken*

I was standin' by the window
On one cold and cloudy day
When I saw the hearse come rolling
For to carry my mother away.

Will the circle be unbroken, by and by, Lord, by and by?
There's a better home a-waiting in the sky, Lord, in the sky.

WATERMELON WINE
**234**

Lord, I told the undertaker
"Undertaker, please drive slow
For this body you are hauling
Lord, I hate to see her go!"

I followed close behind her
Tried to hold up and be brave
But I could not hide my sorrow
When they laid her in the grave.

Went back home, Lord
My home was lonesome
All my brothers, sisters crying
What a home so sad and lone.

*By A.P. Carter. © Copyright 1935
by Peer International Corporation. Copyright renewed. Used by permission.*

\* When the Nitty-Gritty Dirt Band immortalized this song, they titled their album WILL the
Circle Be Unbroken? and most people have sung it that way ever since. A. P. Carter,
however, wrote it as "CAN the Circle Be Unbroken?"

## I'll Be Your San Antone Rose

If they'll play another love song
And if that Miller High Life sign stays dim
And if you'll keep my glass full of whiskey
I'll whisper words I wish I'd said to him.

Just ask me to dance all the slow ones
Hold me close and take me 'cross the floor
I'll gently lay my head on your shoulder
And pretend this never happened before.

I don't want to hear a sad story
We both already know how it goes
So if tonight you'll be my tall dark stranger
I'll be your San Antone Rose

I wish I could tell you I love you
I wish that he weren't always on my mind
If wishes were fast trains to Texas
I'd ride and I'd ride, how I'd ride.

*By Susanna Clark. © Copyright 1975 Sunbury Music, Inc.
Used by permission. All rights reserved.*

## This Is My Year for Mexico

You no longer notice if I'm wearing perfume
I seldom hear a lovin' word from you
Your attention's wrapped up in the morning paper
And I feel a restless yearn for something new

We used to whisper love across the nighttime
Now we never whisper nor recall
Our love is left upon the shelf of winter
Where the sunlight never touches it at all

It's a habit for us to be together
We sit and watch the deadly shadows grow
Everyday last year I left for California
This is my year for Mexico

Your back is turned to me while you are reading
I close my eyes while I pretend to doze
From the road I hear the sound of passing traffic
Some of them are bound for Mexico

It's a habit for us to be together
We sit and watch the deadly shadows grow
Everyday last year I left for California
This is my year for Mexico

*By Vincent Matthews.* © *Copyright Jack Music, Inc.*
*Used by permission. All rights reserved.*

## On Susan's Floor

Like crippled ships that made it
Through the storms and finally reached a quiet shore
The homeless found a home on Susan's floor

I didn't feel so cold and tired
Stretched out before her fire
Rolling smokes and drinkin' of her wine
And I remember candle light and singin' til we could not sing no more
And fallin' warm asleep on Susan's floor

Now that my song is sweeter
I think I'd like to greet her
And thank her for the favors that she gave
A stranger I came

# WATERMELON WINE
## 236

My head bowed in the rain to her door
I sat and sang my songs on Susan's floor

In the morning I'd go off
Buying kingdoms with my songs
Knowing I'd be back in just awhile
Warmin' in the sunlight of her smile

Well lots of time and songs have passed
I catch myself just lookin' back
Reliving all the wonder of those nights
That's where I'd be today
If I had only stayed one night more
And sang another song on Susan's floor

Like crippled ships that made it
Through the storms and finally reached a quiet shore
The homeless found a home on Susan's floor